THE 5:2 FAST DIET COOKBOOK

THE 5:2
FAST DIET
COOKBOOK

150 Easy Fat-Burning Recipes
Under 300 Calories

By Samantha Logan

SKYHORSE PUBLISHING

Skyhorse Publishing books may be purchased in bulk at special discounts for sales promotion, corporate gifts, fund-raising, or educational purposes. Special editions can also be created to specifications. For details, contact the Special Sales Department, Skyhorse Publishing, 307 West 36th Street, 11th Floor, New York, NY 10018 or info@skyhorsepublishing.com.

Skyhorse® and Skyhorse Publishing® are registered trademarks of Skyhorse Publishing, Inc.®, a Delaware corporation.

www.skyhorsepublishing.com

10 9 8 7 6 5 4 3 2 1

Library of Congress Cataloging-in-Publication Data is available on file.

ISBN: 978-1-62636-361-8

Printed in the United States of America

Contents

Introduction: Intermittent Fasting and Why 5:2 Works

If you're like most dieters, you've probably already sampled a bunch of different diets and jumped on the bandwagon for various weight-loss crazes. Maybe you found that they worked well for a while, but then became either unmanageable or too expensive—or, the biggest diet killer of them all, boring.

The 5:2 Diet is different because it really does keep your life as normal as possible. For two days, and not in a row, you need to be extra-specially conscious of what you eat. Otherwise, you're pretty much on your own. You want to eat ice cream or savor a bacon cheeseburger on a non-fast day? That's okay. Have a cocktail on a day you're not fasting? Go for it. The 5:2 Diet takes the part of your dieting life that's about "going without" and condenses it to about 20 percent of your life.

Lose weight working at it only about 20 percent of the time? How can that possibly work? Does it work? The 5:2 Diet targets a very specific component of weight-loss management: metabolism. Causing your body to go without in a regulated fashion actually helps you reset your metabolism and rev up your body's fat-burning ability. When you maximize your body's ability to burn fat, you start losing inches, and mainly in that stubborn mid-section area. And the best part is that while this is all going on, you're only technically "dieting" two days a week, so the deprivation part barely even has time to sink in. Add to this that there are ways (at least 150 in this book) to feel less deprived on those fasting days, and you have a diet you can stick to and get the results you've been craving.

Now you may be thinking that in all the research you've done about losing weight, one of the main ways a person can pretty much guarantee they're *not* going to lose weight is by not eating. The more you understand about fasting and the better you understand it, the more you'll see that fasting isn't starving at all. It's simply a matter of cutting down calories drastically some of the time. While the normal calorie allowance intake for men is about 2,500, and for women, 2,000, the 5:2 Diet calls for 600 calories for men and 500 for women on fast days. But is it even possible to eat enjoyably on that little amount of calories? It is!

If food plays a major role in your enjoyment of life, fasting could actually work well for you. If you can't subsist on protein shakes and carrot sticks, you don't have to. With the 5:2 Diet you can eat food. Real food. Good food. You just have to monitor the calories your foods harbor, and be cautious with how you prepare foods as well as the portions you consume.

Each of the recipes in this book is no more than 300 calories, and many are even less than that. There's even a special dessert section in the back that will give you low-calorie rewards to look forward to on non-fasting days.

Some people enjoy the 5:2 Diet so much, they make it a lifestyle choice to fast one or two days a week, and this isn't a bad thing. Scientific studies have proven that the benefits of fasting go beyond simply shedding excess pounds. An intermittent diet can, among other benefits, delay the onset of Alzheimer's and Parkinson's Disease, and may also prolong your life.

As with any weight-loss plan, it isn't just about what you eat (or don't eat). Yes, you can lose weight on the 5:2 Diet, but you can maximize the weight you lose by adding or upping your exercise. This doesn't mean going to the gym religiously; it could be as simple as deciding to take the stairs instead of the elevator. Parking in the farthest spot away from the store in the parking lot. Walking just half an hour a day. Stick with your plan, add more "steps" to your life, and you too will see results.

I hope the recipes in this book will help you to enjoy satisfying foods on your fasting days, as well as help you make smart food choices on the other days of the week. Reaching for plain or sparkling water instead of a sugary juice or soda, substituting leaner meats for fattier ones. These small steps you take can set you on a road to a healthier, longer-living you.

Chapter 1: Breakfast and Smoothies

On fasting days, you definitely want to make the most of breakfast. The more satisfying this meal, the easier it will be to make it to the next time you eat. That being said, a bowl of fruit salad is a healthy breakfast, but is not likely to sustain you until dinner, so it's not a great choice on a fasting day.

To stave off hunger, make sure your breakfast maximizes protein. Eggs, simply prepared, are excellent sources of protein. Another healthy alternative is smoothies, though you have to be careful with these. While packed with nutrition, smoothies (not the ones included here) have a tendency to shoot up your calorie intake.

Carb-heavy foods like cereal, cereal bars, muffins, toast, and so forth can get very high in calories, though some low-cal recipes for these kinds of foods have been included here, for variety. These types of breakfasts are best for non-fasting mornings.

Broccoli and Gruyere Omelet

Total Calories Per Serving: 179

Nutrient-rich broccoli gets a creamy kick from gruyere cheese in this light yet satisfying omelet. Add a slice of dry homemade whole wheat toast (see page 20) for an additional 70 calories and your calorie count will still be under 250 for the meal!

Makes 1 Omelet

Ingredients

Cooking spray

3 egg whites

1 slice gruyere cheese

½ cup broccoli, chopped

Salt and pepper, to taste

Directions

Step 1: Coat a nonstick skillet with cooking spray and heat on medium.

Step 2: Whisk egg whites in a bowl and pour into heated pan. When edges firm, add cheese to the center. Top with chopped broccoli and sprinkle with salt and pepper.

Step 3: When omelet firms, about 1-2 minutes, use a spatula to fold up the sides to the center, one side at a time. Serve immediately.

Variation

Gruyere is close to Swiss cheese, though it has a nuttier, creamier taste. If you prefer to use Swiss, you'll lose out on that flavor, but you'll save yourself about 10 calories. Also, if you want to use 2 whole eggs instead of 3 egg whites, this will increase your calorie count by about 60 calories.

Nutritional Information

Calories 179		Total Carbohydrates 3.7 g	1%
Calories from Fat 84		Dietary Fiber 1.1 g	5%
	% Daily Value	Sugars 1.6 g	
Total Fat 9.4 g	14%	Protein 20.4 g	
Saturated Fat 5.3 g	27%	Vitamin A	11%
Trans Fat 0		Vitamin C	68%
Cholesterol 31 mg	10%	Calcium	31%
Sodium 273 mg	11%	Iron	3%

Red, Whites, and Green Omelet

Total Calories Per Serving: 217

A yummy, quick, highly nutritional way to start the day. You can add extra salt but you won't need it: The feta cheese should satisfy your salt cravings, and the sautéed shallots add another dimension of flavor.

Makes 1 Omelet

Ingredients

3 cherry tomatoes, chopped
1 teaspoon olive oil
1 tablespoon shallots, minced
¼ cup baby spinach leaves

Cooking spray
3 egg whites
2 tablespoons feta cheese, crumbled

Directions

Step 1: Place chopped tomatoes on a paper towel to absorb excess water.

Step 2: Add olive oil to a skillet and heat on medium. Add shallots and sauté until soft, about 3 minutes. Toss in the spinach and sauté until just wilted, about 1 minute. Set aside.

Step 3: Carefully wipe out skillet with dry paper towel and coat with cooking spray. Add egg whites. When the edges begin to firm, add spinach-shallot mixture, tomatoes, and feta cheese to center of the eggs.

Step 4: When omelet firms, about 1-2 minutes, use a spatula to fold up the sides to the center, one side at a time. Serve immediately.

Nutritional Information

Calories 217		Total Carbohydrates 17.8 g	6%
Calories from Fat 90		Dietary Fiber 4.7 g	19%
	% Daily Value	Sugars 11.1 g	
Total Fat 9.4 g	14%	Protein 17.2 g	
Saturated Fat 3.5 g	18%	Vitamin A	19%
Trans Fat 0		Vitamin C	135%
Cholesterol 17mg	6%	Calcium	11%
Sodium 399 mg	17%	Iron	36%

Better with Bacon Omelet

Total Calories Per Serving: 278

You can have bacon on a diet, even on a fast day. Turkey bacon is still not the *best* for you, but it's scads more healthy than the alternative—and it's tasty, too, without being too greasy. The muenster cheese here makes this omelet more filling, but if you take it out, you'll save yourself 100 calories! Use that calorie allowance for a slice of your homemade whole wheat toast (see page 20) or a big bowl of unsweetened fruit salad!

Makes 1 Omelet

Ingredients

1 egg

2 egg whites

1 teaspoon butter

2 slices cooked turkey bacon, crumbled

1 cup baby spinach

1 slice muenster cheese

Directions

Step 1: Heat a medium-size skillet pan on medium-high heat and melt the butter in the pan.

Step 2: Whisk together egg and egg whites, and pour into the pan when the butter melts.

Step 3: When the edges start to firm, add the muenster cheese to the middle of the eggs, topped by the bacon and baby spinach.

Step 4: When omelet firms, about 1-2 minutes, use a spatula to fold up the sides to the center, one side at a time. Serve immediately.

Nutritional Information

Calories 278		Total Carbohydrates 2.2 g	1%
Calories from Fat 160		Dietary Fiber 0.7 g	3%
	% Daily Value	Sugars 1.2 g	
Total Fat 17.8 g	27%	Protein 26.2 g	
Saturated Fat 9.1 g	46%	Vitamin A	69%
Trans Fat 0		Vitamin C	14%
Cholesterol 221 mg	74%	Calcium	26%
Sodium 638 mg	27%	Iron	10%

Quick Low-Cal, High-Energy Egg "Pockets"

Total Calories Per Serving: 114

Egg whites are a great source of protein. Combined with a handful of high-octane veggies and just enough cheese to bring everything together, you have a perfect little punch of a meal that should hold you a while. And at just 114 calories, you'll even have an allowance for a pretzel rod (37 calories), a mini box of raisins (48 calories), or even a sugar-free fudge ice-pop (35 calories).

Makes 1 "Pocket"

Ingredients

3 egg whites
1 whole egg
Cooking spray
2 tablespoons onions, chopped
¼ cup mushrooms, sliced
¼ cup tomatoes, diced
2 tablespoons shredded part-skim mozzarella cheese
Salt and pepper

Directions

Step 1: In a medium bowl, whisk together egg whites with whole egg.

Step 2: Spray sauté pan. Toss in onions, then mushrooms and tomatoes and cook on medium-high heat until slightly tender, about 5 minutes. Set aside.

Step 3: Re-spray sauté pan. Pour in egg mixture and season with salt and pepper. Cook on medium heat for about 5 minutes then add veggies to one side of the egg mixture. Sprinkle with cheese and fold into an omelet crescent, and then again into a triangle, or "pocket."

Step 4: Carefully remove "pocket" from pan. Plate or pack in foil for eating on-the-go.

Variation

Great, low-calorie substitutions include zucchini, yellow squash, and bell peppers for the vegetables, and crumbled feta for the cheese.

Nutritional Information

Calories 114		Total Carbohydrates 5.1 g	2%
Calories from Fat 33		Dietary Fiber 1.1 g	4%
	% Daily Value	Sugars 2.9 g	
Total Fat 3.7 g	6%	Protein 15.5 g	
Saturated Fat 1.9 g	9%	Vitamin A	2%
Trans Fat 0		Vitamin C	17%
Cholesterol 8 mg	3%	Calcium	11%
Sodium 242 mg	10%	Iron	7%

Yummy Lo-Cal Breakfast Burritos

Total Calories Per Serving: 240

Make fasting a "fiesta" with yummy breakfast burritos. Fresh cilantro and chunky salsa kick up the standard egg sandwich. To further trim the calorie count, try reducing the cheese by 1 tablespoon, or using 2 egg whites instead of one whole egg.

Makes 1 Burrito

Ingredients

1 large egg
½ teaspoon fresh cilantro, chopped
Salt and pepper
Cooking spray
½ teaspoon butter
2 tablespoons reduced-fat cheddar cheese, shredded
1 fat-free flour toruntila
½ medium tomato, chopped
1 tablespoon chunky salsa

Directions

Step 1: In a bowl, whisk together the egg and cilantro with salt and pepper.

Step 2: Coat a nonstick skillet with cooking spray. Heat on medium and add butter. Add the egg mixture and cook to desired texture, about three to five minutes. Set aside.

Step 3: Carefully wipe out the skillet with a paper towel and spray with cooking spray. Heat the toruntila, about 30 seconds per side. Set aside.

Step 4: Add the cheese to the toruntila, sprinkling evenly down the center. Pour the scrambled egg mixture over the cheese, and top with the tomato and salsa.

Step 5: Fold up the bottom of the tortilla, then fold up the sides to cross the center. Eat immediately or roll in aluminum foil to eat on-the-go.

Variation

Substitute fresh spinach for the tomato to add more green to the burrito, without adding more calories. Part-skim shredded mozzarella has about the same amount of calories as reduced-fat cheddar cheese, and makes a more mild-tasting burrito.

Nutritional Information

Calories 240		Total Carbohydrates 21.2 g	7%
Calories from Fat 94		Dietary Fiber 3.7 g	15%
	% Daily Value	Sugars 0.9 g	
Total Fat 10.5 g	16%	Protein 14.6 g	
Saturated Fat 4.6 g	23%	Vitamin A	10%
Trans Fat 0		Vitamin C	1%
Cholesterol 201 mg	67%	Calcium	23%
Sodium 635 mg	26%	Iron	9%

Black Bean Breakfast Burrito

Total Calories Per Serving: 241

Here's another take on having a "South of the Border" breakfast—this time incorporating black beans into the mix for extra doses of protein, fiber, antioxidants, and Omega 3s.

Makes 1 Burrito

Ingredients

Cooking spray
3 egg whites
¼ cup canned black beans, rinsed and dried

1 ounce no-fat cheddar cheese, shredded
1 fat-free toruntila
2 tablespoons salsa

Directions

Step 1: Heat a skillet pan on medium heat and coat with cooking spray.

Step 2: Whisk egg whites in a bowl and pour into skillet. Allow egg whites to firm for about a minute and add beans and cheese to the eggs and cook until cheese melts. Set aside.

Step 3: Spray the same skillet with cooking spray and place toruntila in skillet, warming about 30 seconds per side.

Step 4: Fill toruntila with egg white, bean, and cheese mixture, then top with salsa. Fold burrito-style and serve.

Variation

If you worry about what to do with the leftover yolks, and instead decide to use 2 whole eggs instead of 3 egg whites in this recipe, you'll shoot right over your calorie allowance. Don't worry about wasting all those extra egg yolks, though. You can save them for non-fast days!

Nutritional Information

Calories 241			Dietary Fiber 5.7 g	23%
Calories from Fat 16			Sugars 2.4 g	
	% Daily Value		Protein 26.9 g	
Total Fat 1.8 g	3%		Vitamin A	10%
Trans Fat 0			Vitamin C	1%
Cholesterol 5mg	2%		Calcium	31%
Sodium 648 mg	27%		Iron	10%
Total Carbohydrates 29.5 g	10%			

THE 5:2 FAST DIET COOKBOOK

"Smokey" Egg Scramble with Salmon and Spinach

Total Calories Per Serving: 219

Smoked salmon is a great breakfast on a bagel slathered with lots of cream cheese, but you'll be eating your entire calorie allowance and then some with a choice like that! Here's a high-protein, low-calorie alternative to having your smoked salmon ... and eating it, too.

Makes 6 servings

Ingredients
4 teaspoons olive oil
1 cup chopped fresh spinach
5 large eggs
¼ teaspoon freshly ground black pepper
3 ounces thinly sliced smoked salmon, diced
4 ounces reduced-fat cream cheese, cut into small cubes
3 whole wheat English muffins, split and toasted

Directions
Step 1: Heat 2 teaspoons olive oil in nonstick skillet over medium heat. Toss in the spinach and sauté just until it wilts. Drain and set aside.

Step 2: In a medium bowl, whisk together eggs and pepper. Add remaining 2 teaspoons of olive oil to skillet, then eggs, and cook until mixture begins to thicken, about 30 seconds.

Step 3: Add salmon and cream cheese to the skillet and cook an additional 30 seconds. Next, stir in the sautéed spinach and cook an additional two minutes, now stirring constantly.

Step 4: Slice each English muffin half in two, and top each with ½ cup egg mixture. Serve immediately.

Continued . . .

Variation

Consider using kale in place of spinach to up the protein and calcium quotient of your breakfast, and boost vitamins C, A, and K. The downside is that kale has about twice the calories of spinach (which will add about 10 calories to the meal).

Nutritional Information

Calories 219		Dietary Fiber 2.3 g	9%
Calories from Fat 107		Sugars 3.7 g	
	% Daily Value	Protein 11.6 g	
Total Fat 11.9 g	18%	Vitamin A	15%
Saturated Fat 4.3 g	22%	Vitamin C	2%
Cholesterol 168mg	56%	Calcium	12%
Sodium 558mg	23%	Iron	10%
Total Carbohydrates 15.2 g	5%		

Spicy Sweet Potato Hash

Total Calories Per Serving: 194

If you're a fan of hash for breakfast, here's a variation on the usual corned-beef hash that's a fraction of the calories and bursting with different flavors. Try this and you might never go back! Top with a poached egg for an additional 70 calories. A whole scrambled egg adds about 100 calories, while 2 scrambled egg whites adds about 35 extra calories.

Makes 2 Servings

Ingredients

2 teaspoons olive oil
1 chili pepper, minced
1 small onion, diced
1 stalk celery, diced
1 clove garlic, minced
1 cup sweet potatoes, peeled, diced, and pre-cooked

¼ cup black beans, drained and rinsed
2 tablespoons salsa
2 tablespoons cilantro, chopped
Salt and pepper, to taste

Directions

Step 1: Heat olive oil in a pan and add chili pepper, onions, celery, and garlic. Sauté and soften about 5 minutes.

Step 2: Add pre-cooked sweet potatoes and beans, and cook an additional 5 minutes.

Step 3: Remove from heat and stir in salsa and cilantro. Season with salt and pepper and serve.

Nutritional Information

Calories 194			Dietary Fiber 8 g	32%
Calories from Fat 5			Sugars 3.1 g	
	% Daily Value		Protein 17.2 g	
Total Fat 0.5 g	1%		Vitamin A	6%
Cholesterol 0mg	0%		Vitamin C	30%
Sodium 112mg	5%		Calcium	5%
Total Carbohydrates 41.2 g	14%			

Egg-Citing Herb Frittata

Total Calories Per Serving: 193

Your choice of herb or herb combination will carry the show in this simple frittata. Use a combination of basil, rosemary, and thyme, or just use your favorite herb for a light, flavorful meal. (If you prefer to use whole eggs, add 60 calories to your total.)

Makes 1 serving

Ingredients

1 teaspoon extra-virgin olive oil

1 cup diced onion

4 egg whites

2 teaspoons chopped fresh herbs

⅛ teaspoon salt

⅛ teaspoon freshly ground pepper

2 tablespoons part-skim ricotta

Directions

Step 1: Warm olive oil in a large nonstick skillet over medium-high heat and add onion. Sauté onion about 5 minutes, until it softens and begins to brown.

Step 2: Whisk egg whites together in a small bowl and pour into skillet with the onion. Cook egg and onion mixture about a minute, stirring occasionally, while the egg becomes firm.

Step 3: Top frittata with chopped herbs and then ricotta cheese. Continue cooking an additional 2 minutes or so, until the cheese begins to melt. Season with salt and pepper. Serve immediately.

Nutritional Information

	% Daily Value			
Calories 193		Total Carbohydrates 13.1 g	4%
Calories from Fat 66		Dietary Fiber 2.4 g	10%
	% Daily Value	Sugars 5.6 g	
Total Fat 7.4 g	11%	Protein 19.2 g	
Saturated Fat 2.2 g	11%	Vitamin A	4%
Trans Fat 0		Vitamin C	20%
Cholesterol 10mg	3%	Calcium	10%
Sodium 551mg	23%	Iron	2%

Make-Ahead Ham-n-Cheese

Total Calories Per Serving: 266

Ham-n-cheese on a diet? You bet! Here's a filling new take on classic ham-n-cheese that makes a great, satisfying breakfast but could easily work as a dinner option as well. Just serve with a small green salad dressed in nothing but a squeeze of fresh lemon juice (15 calories for both!) and you'll still be well within your calorie allotment.

Makes 8 servings

Ingredients
¾ cup fat-free buttermilk
2 large egg whites
2 cups all-purpose flour
1 tablespoon baking powder
2 teaspoons sugar
¼ teaspoon salt
¼ teaspoon ground red pepper
3 tablespoons chilled butter
¾ cup shredded reduced-fat extra-sharp cheddar cheese
¾ cup finely chopped 33%-less-sodium ham
Cooking spray

Directions
Step 1: Preheat oven to 400°.
Step 2: In a medium bowl, whisk together buttermilk and egg whites. Set aside.
Step 3: Next, lightly toss together flour, baking powder, sugar, salt, and pepper in an electric mixing bowl. Using a low speed, cut in and add butter, blending until the mixture becomes coarse.
Step 3: Remove bowl from stand and stir in cheese and ham, then fold in buttermilk and egg white mixture, turning until moist.
Step 4: On a lightly floured surface, lightly knead dough 4 to 5 times and shape into an 8-inch circle on a baking sheet coated with cooking spray. Cut the dough into 8 wedges without cutting all the way through.
Step 5: Bake at 400° for 20 minutes or until lightly browned. Cool before serving.

Continued . . .

Variation

Use turkey ham instead of regular low-sodium ham and save yourself approximately 60 more calories right there.

Nutritional Information

Calories 266		Total Carbohydrates 28.1 g	9%
Calories from Fat 94		Dietary Fiber 0.9 g	4%
	% Daily Value	Sugars 2.7 g	
Total Fat 10.4 g	16%	Protein 13.6 g	
Saturated Fat 5.9 g	29%	Vitamin A	8%
Trans Fat 0		Vitamin C	1%
Cholesterol 40mg	13%	Calcium	27%
Sodium 518mg	22%	Iron	11%

Pizza for Breakfast!

Total Calories Per Serving: 279

Who says you can't have pizza for breakfast? Pizza lovers will love this clever take on their favorite food.

Makes 1 Pizza

Ingredients

1 large egg

Cooking spray

1 whole-wheat English muffin

2 tablespoons marinara sauce

2 tablespoons mozzarella cheese

2 slices turkey pepperoni

Preparation

Step 1: Preheat oven or toaster oven to 350°. Split and toast English muffin and whisk egg in a small bowl.

Step 2: Heat a small skillet coated in cooking spray over medium-high heat and add egg. Cook about 2-3 minutes, stirring occasionally.

Step 3: On each toasted English muffin half, spread 1 tablespoon of marinara sauce and divide scrambled eggs between the two. Place a slice of pepperoni on each and top with the cheese.

Step 4: Heat in oven or toaster oven until the cheese is melted, about 3-5 minutes. Serve immediately.

Nutritional Information

Calories 279		Total Carbohydrates 32.5 g	11%
Calories from Fat 84		Dietary Fiber 2.3 g	9%
	% Daily Value	Sugars 2.5 g	
Total Fat 9.3 g	14%	Protein 16.6 g	
Saturated Fat 4 g	20%	Vitamin A	7%
Trans Fat 0		Vitamin C	2%
Cholesterol 198mg	11%	Calcium	24%
Sodium 1306mg	54%	Iron	20%

"Fast"-Friendly French Toast

Total Calories Per Serving: 216

Forget the thick challah bread French toast—slathered in butter and oozing with maple syrup—that you might order in a diner. Yes, it's delicious, but just the French toast, plain, is over 360 calories! Here's a variation that's both healthy and quite filling. (And if you need to "top the toast," try topping with ¼ cup blueberries, ¼ cup sliced strawberries, and ¼ cup sliced banana—which adds only 66 calories.)

Makes 2 servings

Ingredients
Cooking spray
3 large eggs
¼ cup 1% milk
1 teaspoon ground cinnamon
4 slices of reduced-calorie whole wheat bread

Directions
Step 1: Coat a griddle or a large skillet with cooking spray and heat on medium to high heat.

Step 2: While your cooking surface heats, whisk together the eggs, milk, and cinnamon in a bowl.

Step 3: Soak both sides of each slice of bread in the egg and milk mixture and place on the hot griddle or skillet. Cook until the toast is firm and nicely browned, about a minute and a half per side. Serve immediately.

Variation
Not a fan of whole wheat bread for French toast? You'll lose some of the nutritional value, but you can make this recipe with reduced-calorie white instead. It will add about 20 calories to your total intake, which still keeps you in the right range.

Nutritional Information

Calories 216		Total Carbohydrates 23.1 g	8%
Calories from Fat 82		Dietary Fiber 6.1 g	25%
	% Daily Value	Sugars 3.6 g	
Total Fat 9.1 g	14%	Protein 14.7 g	
Saturated Fat 2.7 g	14%	Vitamin A	9%
Trans Fat 0		Vitamin C	0%
Cholesterol 281 mg	94%	Calcium	12%
Sodium 354 mg	15%	Iron	16%

Cinnamon Swirl Pancakes

Total Calories Per Serving: 298

Reminiscent of cinnamon toast, these pancakes are fun and flavorful. The calorie count is edging to the top of the 300-calorie allowance, but this count is based on enjoying 2 pancakes. Cut it dramatically by having only one pancake and topping it with fresh, yummy berries or apple slices.

Makes 8 pancakes

Ingredients

Cooking spray

2 cups whole wheat flour

1 teaspoon baking soda

2 medium eggs

1 cup nonfat milk

1 tablespoon vanilla extract

2 tablespoons ground cinnamon

Directions

Step 1: Heat a large skillet over medium-high heat and spray with cooking spray. If you're using a griddle, heat to high and coat with cooking spray.

Step 2: In a medium bowl, mix together the flour and baking soda. In another bowl, lightly whisk together eggs, milk, and vanilla extract, then pour into dry ingredients and fold together. Swirl in cinnamon.

Step 3: Pour circles of pancake batter into skillet or onto griddle and cook 1-2 minutes, or until the edges of the pancakes begin to firm and the batter in the middle starts to bubble slightly. Flip and cook another minute or so. Serve immediately.

Nutritional Information

Calories 298		Total Carbohydrates 54	18%
Calories from Fat 26		Dietary Fiber 3.5 g	14%
	% Daily Value	Sugars 3.9 g	
Total Fat 2.9 g	4%	Protein 11.4 g	
Saturated Fat 0.8 g	4%	Vitamin A	5%
Trans Fat 0		Vitamin C	0
Cholesterol 83mg	28%	Calcium	13%
Sodium 373mg	16%	Iron	20%

Cran-Tastic Pancakes

Total Calories Per Serving: 197

Savory and tart, cranberry is a great "wake-up" for the tastebuds, but these flavor-bursting berries are also incredibly healthy. They have less calories than other berries (a half cup of cranberries contains about 25 calories), and they're slightly higher in vitamin C.

Makes 2 to 3 pancakes

Ingredients

¼ cup fresh cranberries, boiled, drained, and coarsely chopped

2 tablespoons all-purpose flour

1 tablespoon plus 1 teaspoon whole wheat flour

½ tablespoon yellow cornmeal

½ tablespoon sugar

½ teaspoon baking powder

Pinch of salt

Pinch of ground nutmeg

6 tablespoons nonfat milk

1 large egg white

1 teaspoon vegetable oil

Directions

Step 1: In a large bowl, whisk together the dry ingredients, through nutmeg.

Step 2: In a separate bowl, mix together the milk, egg white, and oil, and pour into the dry mixture. With a rubber spatula, gently fold in the cranberries.

Step 3: Heat a large nonstick skillet or frying pan, coated with cooking oil, over medium heat and coat with cooking oil. Pour circles of batter into pan or skillet.

Step 4: Cook pancakes about 2 minutes, or until the edges firm and turn slightly golden. Flip and continue cooking an additional minute or two. Serve immediately.

Nutritional Information

	% Daily Value		
Calories 197		Total Carbohydrates 30.3 g	10%
Calories from Fat 46		Dietary Fiber 1.9 g	8%
		Sugars 12.3 g	
Total Fat 51.1 g	8%	Protein 8.7 g	
Saturated Fat 1.1 g	5%	Vitamin A	4%
Trans Fat 0		Vitamin C	5%
Cholesterol 2mg	1%	Calcium	23%
Sodium 253mg	11%	Iron	7%

Homemade Whole Wheat Toast with Flavorful Toppers

Homemade Whole Wheat Bread Toast (2 slices) Total Calories Per Serving: 150
Apple "Butter" (2 Tablespoons) Total Calories Per Serving: 50
Orange Fig Jam (2 Tablespoons) Total Calories Per Serving: 75
Pumpkin "Butter" (2 Tablespoons) Total Calories Per Serving: 22

Toast and butter or jam is a quick, out-the-door-in-a-hurry breakfast staple, but slather a couple of slices of regular whole wheat bread with a couple of tablespoons of regular butter and you're looking at almost 500 calories! (An Egg McMuffin from McDonald's clocks in at about 300 calories.) On a Sunday, take the time to bake a loaf of whole wheat bread yourself, and whip up these flavorful "butters" to top them with for a breakfast that will leave you as satisfied as an Egg McMuffin might, without all the salt and fat.

Homemade Whole Wheat Bread

Makes approximately 12–14 slices

Ingredients

3 cups whole wheat bread flour

1¾ cups nonfat milk

2 tablespoons light olive oil

1 tablespoon agave nectar

1 package instant yeast

1 teaspoon sea salt

Cooking spray

Directions

Step 1: Mix flour, milk, olive oil, agave, yeast, and salt in the bowl of a stand mixer using the dough attachment on slow-to-medium setting for about 2 minutes. If you chose to knead the dough by hand, mix all ingredients in a large bowl until they come together as a dough. Lightly flour your hands and kneading surface, and knead for about 8 minutes.

Step 2: Roll the dough into a ball. Cover with light sprinkle of flour to prevent sticking. Lightly tent the dough with plastic wrap and let rise one and a half hours, until it's doubled in size.

Step 3: With hands floured, press dough back down in the bowl and let sit 15 minutes. Remove and place on floured surface.

Step 4: Roll out dough into the shape of a rectangle, 1-inch thick. Fold the dough over long, with the ends meeting in the middle. Pinch dough ends together. Fold over short ends and pinch to flaps already folded over.

Step 5: Preheat oven to 350°. Coat a loaf pan with cooking spray and flip dough over into the pan, seam side down. Sprinkle with flour and lightly cover with plastic wrap or a dry towel. Allow dough to rise to 1 inch above top of pan.

Step 6: Carefully remove towel or wrap and with a sharp knife, slice the top of the loaf lengthwise. Place in oven and bake 45 minutes, until the bread is golden brown, misting the oven with a spray bottle every 5 to 10 minutes.

Step 7: Remove from oven and let loaf pan cool. Remove loaf from pan and cool bread on a wire rack. Slice and serve.

Nutritional Information

Calories 150		Total Carbohydrates 27.2 g	9%
Calories from Fat 25		Dietary Fiber 1.0 g	4%
	% Daily Value	Sugars 3.2g	
Total Fat 2.7g	4%	Protein 4.6g	
Saturated Fat 0		Vitamin A	1%
Trans Fat 0		Vitamin C	0%
Cholesterol 1mg	0%	Calcium	5%
Sodium 22.7g	7%	Iron	9%

Apple "Butter"

Makes about 1 cup of apple butter, or 8 2-tablespoon servings

Ingredients

3 apples, peeled and cored
1 cup apple juice
½ cup water
Pinch of cinnamon
Pinch of nutmeg

Directions

Step 1: Preheat oven to 350°.

Step 2: Chop apples into half-inch chunks and place in a roasting pan. Pour apple juice and water over the apples, and sprinkle with cinnamon and nutmeg.

Step 3: Bake for 60 minutes, or until soft. If they're not tender after 60 minutes, continue baking, checking every 15 minutes.

Step 4: Remove from oven and mash soft apples with a potato masher or fork. Return to oven and bake an additional 10-15 minutes, until apple butter turns golden brown. Cool and serve.

Nutritional Information

Calories 50		Total Carbohydrates 13.1 g	4%
Calories from Fat 0		Dietary Fiber 1.7 g	7%
	% Daily Value	Sugars 10.5 g	
Total Fat 0		Protein 0 g	
Saturated Fat 0		Vitamin A	1%
Trans Fat 0		Vitamin C	27%
Cholesterol 0		Calcium	1%
Sodium 2mg	0%	Iron	1%

Orange-Fig Jam

Makes 32 2-tablespoon servings

Ingredients

1¾ cups water

1½ cups sugar

¼ cup Grand Marnier

¼ cup fresh orange juice

14 ounces dried Calimyrna figs, coarsely chopped

1 teaspoon grated orange rind

Directions

Step 1: In a large saucepan, dissolve sugar in water, Grand Marnier, and orange juice over medium heat. When sugar is dissolved, add figs and bring to a boil.

Step 2: Set to simmer and sprinkle in orange rind. Cover and cook 2 ½ to 3 hours, until liquid reduces by half or more.

Step 3: Pour mixture into a bowl and allow to cool about ½ hour.

Step 4: Now pour cooled mixture into a blender or food processor, blending until smooth. Chill and serve.

Nutritional Information

Calories 75		Total Carbohydrates 17.2 g	6%
Calories from Fat 0		Dietary Fiber 1.5 g	6%
	% Daily Value	Sugars 16.9 g	
Total Fat 0		Protein 0.3 g	
Saturated Fat 0		Vitamin A	3%
Trans Fat 0		Vitamin C	56%
Cholesterol 0		Calcium	59%
Sodium 147mg	6%	Iron	56%

Pumpkin "Butter"

Makes about 3 cups of pumpkin butter

Ingredients

15 ounces canned pumpkin purée
1 cup applesauce
⅓ cup light brown sugar, packed
¾ teaspoon ground cinnamon
¼ teaspoon ground ginger
2 tablespoons fresh lemon juice

Directions

Step 1: Stir together pumpkin, applesauce, sugar, cinnamon, and ginger in a sauce pan and heat over medium heat.
Step 2: Bring the mixture to a boil. Then reduce heat immediately.
Step 3: Simmer, stirring often, until mixture becomes thick, about 45 minutes.
Step 4: Remove from heat and stir in lemon juice. Cool and serve.

Nutritional Information

Calories 22		Total Carbohydrates 5.6 g	2%
Calories from Fat 1		Dietary Fiber 0.8 g	3%
	% Daily Value	Sugars 4.3 g	
Total Fat 0		Protein 0.3 g	
Saturated Fat 0		Vitamin A	66%
Trans Fat 0		Vitamin C	3%
Cholesterol 0		Calcium	1%
Sodium 2mg	0%	Iron	2%

Sugar-Free Bran Muffins

Total Calories Per Serving: 110

The natural sugars in raisins and bananas, plus the sweetness of buttermilk, brings a lovely and satisfying sweetness to these muffins, and means not having to add extra sugar—and extra calories.

Makes 12 muffins

Ingredients

Cooking spray (optional)
1½ cups whole wheat flour
1½ cups unprocessed Miller's natural bran
2 teaspoons baking soda
1 tablespoon cinnamon
1 teaspoon nutmeg

½ cup golden raisins
3 egg whites
½ cup buttermilk
½ cup water
1 small ripe banana, mashed
1 teaspoon vanilla extract
½ teaspoon banana extract

Directions

Step 1: Preheat oven to 400°. Spray muffin tins with cooking spray or line with paper or foil muffin cups, and set aside.

Step 2: In a large bowl, mix together the flour, bran, baking soda, cinnamon, nutmeg, and raisins. Set aside.

Step 3: In another bowl, whisk egg whites and stir in buttermilk, water, mashed banana and vanilla and banana extracts.

Step 4: Fold egg mixture into dry ingredients and stir until combined.

Step 5: Spoon mixture into muffin cups and bake 15 minutes. Remove from oven and cool. Serve warm.

Nutritional Information

Calories 110		Total Carbohydrates 23.8 g	8%
Calories from Fat 6		Dietary Fiber 3.9 g	15%
	% Daily Value	Sugars 5.3 g	
Total Fat 0.7 g	1%	Protein 4.1 g	
Saturated Fat 0		Vitamin A	0%
Trans Fat 0		Vitamin C	2%
Cholesterol 0		Calcium	3%
Sodium 237mg	10%	Iron	9%

Apple Oatmeal Muffins

Total Calories Per Serving: 175

Makes 12 muffins

Ingredients

Cooking spray (optional)
1½ cups apple juice
2 teaspoons vanilla extract
½ cup sugar
1½ cups quick oats
1½ cups whole wheat flour

2 teaspoons baking powder
2 medium apples, grated
1 teaspoon cinnamon
4 egg whites, beaten to soft
   peaks

Directions

Step 1: Preheat oven to 400°. Spray muffin tin with cooking spray, or line with paper or foil muffin cups.

Step 2: In a medium-sized bowl, mix apple juice with vanilla extract and sugar, and stir in the oats. Soak oats in liquid and sugar for 30 minutes.

Step 3: In a separate bowl, mix together the flour, baking powder, grated apple, and cinnamon. Fold in to wet ingredients.

Step 4: In another bowl, whisk the egg whites and then fold in with other ingredients.

Step 5: Pour the mixture into the muffin cups and bake 25-30 minutes, until muffins are golden brown. Remove from oven and cool in pan. Remove and cool further on rack. Serve warm.

Nutritional Information

Calories 175		Total Carbohydrates 37.8 g	13%
Calories from Fat 8		Dietary Fiber 2.7 g	11%
	% Daily Value	Sugars 16.7 g	
Total Fat 0.09 g	1%	Protein 4.2 g	
Saturated Fat 0		Vitamin A	1%
Trans Fat 0		Vitamin C	25%
Cholesterol 0		Calcium	5%
Sodium 21mg	1%	Iron	8%

Savory-Sweet Oatmeal

Total Calories Per Serving: 194

Oatmeal for breakfast is boring no more with some yummy, crunchy adds. But the fruit and nuts aside, one of the best parts of this breakfast is the ground flaxseed. High in protein and fiber, this grain is also high in Omega 3s, which helps with weight loss and lowers cholesterol.

Makes 6 ⅔ cup servings

Ingredients

3 cups fat-free milk
1½ cups regular oats
1½ cups Granny Smith apple (about 1 medium), diced
1 tablespoon ground flaxseed
½ teaspoon ground cinnamon
¼ teaspoon salt

½ teaspoon vanilla extract
3 tablespoons brown sugar
3 tablespoons roasted almonds, slivered
¼ cup hazelnuts, roasted and finely chopped

Directions

Step 1: In a large saucepan, combine milk, oats, apple, flaxseed, cinnamon, and salt, and heat on medium.

Step 2: Bring to a boil. Stir in vanilla extract and reduce heat to simmer for approximately 5 minutes, or until oatmeal is thick.

Step 3: Remove from heat and fold in brown sugar and nuts. Spoon into bowls and serve warm.

Variation

If flaxseed does not agree with you, you may try substituting with wheat germ, which is a great source of folic acid and antioxidants. It also has slightly fewer calories than flaxseed, though not all the benefits. Oat germ is also high in antioxidants and soluble fiber, and has slightly fewer calories than both flaxseed and wheat germ.

Nutritional Information

Calories 194		Total Carbohydrates 29.4 g	10%
Calories from Fat 46		Dietary Fiber 3.9 g	16%
	% Daily Value	Sugars 13.9 g	
Total Fat 5.2 g	8%	Protein 8.3 g	
Saturated Fat 0.6 g	3%	Vitamin A	5%
Trans Fat 0		Vitamin C	2%
Cholesterol 2mg	1%	Calcium	19%
Sodium 152mg	6%	Iron	7%

Superfoods Trifecta in a Bowl!

Total Calories Per Serving: 201

Quinoa, blueberries, and walnuts, all proven "superfoods," come together for a luscious, enjoyable breakfast that won't break your calorie ceiling!

Makes about 2 cups

Ingredients

½ cup quinoa, raw
1 cup almond milk, unsweetened
¼ cup fresh blueberries
1 tablespoon chopped walnuts
Dash of cinnamon

Directions

Step 1: Place quinoa in a fine mesh strainer. Rinse and drain quinoa.

Step 2: Combine quinoa and milk in a medium saucepan. Bring to boiling.

Step 3: Cover and reduce heat to a gentle simmer. Cook 10 to 15 minutes until the water is absorbed and the quinoa is tender.

Step 4: Add walnuts and cinnamon. Let cool. Add fresh blueberries on top.

Nutritional Information

Calories 201			Total Carbohydrates 29.7 g	10%
Calories from Fat 60			Dietary Fiber 4 g	16%
		% Daily Value	Sugars 1.9 g	
Total Fat 6.6 g		10%	Protein 6.9 g	
Saturated Fat 0.5 g		3%	Vitamin A	5%
Trans Fat 0			Vitamin C	3%
Cholesterol 0			Calcium	16%
Sodium 87mg		4%	Iron	15%

A Muesli Medley

Total Calories Per Serving: 191

Muesli is a crunchy treat that sasses up a basic breakfast of plain yogurt and fruit in this bountiful, filling breakfast.

Makes 1 ¼ cups

Ingredients
  ½ cup nonfat plain yogurt
  Drizzle of honey or pure maple syrup
  ¼ cup unsweetened muesli
  ½ cup fresh berries
  ¼ cup diced apple
  ¼ cup diced banana

Directions
Step 1: Pour yogurt into a bowl. Drizzle in honey or maple syrup and gently mix.
Step 2: Fold in museli and then fruit and serve.

Nutritional Information

	% Daily Value		
Calories 191		Total Carbohydrates 35.2 g	12%
Calories from Fat 17		Dietary Fiber 4.2 g	17%
		Sugars 26.8 g	
Total Fat 1.9 g	3%	Protein 7.9 g	
Saturated Fat 1.3 g	6%	Vitamin A	3%
Trans Fat 0		Vitamin C	34%
Cholesterol 7 mg	2%	Calcium	24%
Sodium 87 mg	4%	Iron	3%

"Healthy Candy" Parfait

Total Calories Per Serving: 163

Are all sweets bad for you? Not when it comes to this creamy parfait, made with a base of Greek yogurt and incorporating delicious super-foods like dark chocolate, granola, walnuts, and wild blueberries. It's like eating your favorite fruit-and-nut candy bar with a spoon. And at under 200 calories, it's nothing you need to feel guilty about!

Makes 4 parfaits

Ingredients
½ cup fresh blueberries
2 cups nonfat Greek yogurt
2½ tablespoons organic dark-chocolate chips
¼ cup oat granola
¼ cup chopped walnuts

Directions
Step 1: Arrange 4 parfait glasses on your counter and spoon 1 table-spoon of the blueberries into each glass.
Step 2: On top of the blueberries, add ¼ cup nonfat Greek-style yogurt in each glass.
Step 3: Top the yogurt with 1 teaspoon mini dark-chocolate chips, 1 tablespoon oat granola, and a sprinkling of chopped walnuts each, then add another layer of the berries, yogurt, chocolate, walnuts, and granola to each. Serve immediately.

Variation
Looking to make this treat slightly more filling? Slice up a banana and layer the slices into the mix, adding approximately 25 calories to each parfait, but lots of extra potassium, vitamins C and B6, and fiber.

Nutritional Information

	% Daily Value		
Calories 163		Total Carbohydrates 15.5 g	5%
Calories from Fat 56		Dietary Fiber 1.5 g	6%
		Sugars 9.5 g	
Total Fat 6.2 g	10%	Protein 14.6 g	
Saturated Fat 1.1 g	5%	Vitamin A	0
Trans Fat 0		Vitamin C	4%
Cholesterol 5mg	2%	Calcium	16%
Sodium 58mg	2%	Iron	4%

Peachy Keen Parfait

Total Calories Per Serving: 216

Peaches-n-cream never tasted better than they do in this sweet and satisfying parfait. If you'd prefer to use cottage cheese in place of the yogurt, you can, adding only another 40 calories.

Makes 1 parfait

Ingredients
    1 cup fat-free plain yogurt
    2 teaspoons toasted wheat germ
    1 cup chopped peach or nectarine (about 2)

Directions
Step 1: Mix wheat germ into yogurt.
Step 2: Place half the fruit in a bowl. Top with the yogurt-wheat germ mixture, then top with the rest of the fruit. Serve.

Nutritional Information

Calories 216		Dietary Fiber 3.1 g	12%
Calories from Fat 12		Sugars 30.1 g	
	% Daily Value	Protein 16.9 g	
Total Fat 1.4 g	2%	Vitamin A	10%
Cholesterol 5mg	2%	Vitamin C	17%
Sodium 189mg	8%	Calcium	50%
Total Carbohydrates 35.7 g	12%	Iron	6%

"Pumpkin Pie" Parfait

Total Calories Per Serving: 269

Get the pleasure of having pumpkin pie for breakfast without the guilt. The granola makes for a healthy "faux" crust, and the honey gives it just enough sweetness.

Makes 1 serving

Ingredients
¾ cup plain low-fat yogurt
2 teaspoons honey
¼ cup canned pumpkin
Pinch of pumpkin spice
⅛ cup Granola

Directions
Step 1: In a mixing bowl, mix together the yogurt, honey, and pumpkin spice.
Step 2: Layer half the pumpkin, then the yogurt, then the granola into a cereal bowl. Repeat and serve.

Nutritional Information

Calories 269		Total Carbohydrates 37.7 g	13%
Calories from Fat 55		Dietary Fiber 3.2 g	13%
	% Daily Value	Sugars 29.5 g	
Total Fat 6.1 g	9%	Protein 13.4 g	
Saturated Fat 2.6 g	13%	Vitamin A	193%
Trans Fat		Vitamin C	7%
Cholesterol 11mg	4%	Calcium	37%
Sodium 136mg	6%	Iron	10%

Peruvian Parfait

Total Calories Per Serving: 238

Popular in Peru and throughout Latin America, mango and papaya, together with quinoa, come together here to make for a delicious, guilt-free Latin-inspired dessert—for breakfast.

Makes 1 cup

Ingredients

⅓ cup nonfat plain yogurt

⅓ cup quinoa, cooked

¼ cup of mango chunks

¼ cup papaya chunks

Directions

Step 1: Spoon half the yogurt into a bowl.

Step 2: Add the quinoa, then the fruit. Served chilled.

Nutritional Information

Calories 238		Total Carbohydrates 41.4 g	14%
Calories from Fat 29		Dietary Fiber 4.4 g	18%
	% Daily Value	Sugars 13.4 g	
Total Fat 3.2 g	5%	Protein 9.7 g	
Saturated Fat 0.9 g	5%	Vitamin A	15%
Trans Fat 0		Vitamin C	57%
Cholesterol 4mg	1%	Calcium	14%
Sodium 46mg	2%	Iron	11%

Tropical Paradise Smoothie

Total Calories Per Serving: 292

This smoothie is a lime lover's Pina Colada, but without the rum. The coconut milk is creamy and satisfying. If you want to make this smoothie more of a slushie, add a cup of ice.

Makes 2 Smoothies

Ingredients

1 medium lime, peeled and sliced
¼ cup raspberries
⅔ cup unsweetened coconut milk
⅔ cup fat-free lime sherbet
¼ cup pineapple juice

Directions

Step 1: Add all the ingredients together in a blender.
Step 2: Blend on high speed until all the fruit chunks are liquified.

Variation

If you're not a fan of coconut milk, substitute it with unsweetened almond milk. You'll lose that "tropical" feel, but you'll save yourself about 15 calories. If you'd prefer to go with a different kind of berry, strawberries and blackberries have slightly fewer calories than raspberries, while blueberries have slightly more. If you go with blueberries, add less lime sherbet or eliminate the pineapple juice.

Nutritional Information

Calories 292		Total Carbohydrates 30.5 g	10%
Calories from Fat 174		Dietary Fiber 3.8 g	15%
	% Daily Value	Sugars 20.4 g	
Total Fat 19.3 g	30%	Protein 2.4 g	
Saturated Fat 16.9	85%	Vitamin A	0%
Trans Fat 0		Vitamin C	32%
Cholesterol 0		Calcium	5%
Sodium 33mg	1%	Iron	10%

Protein-Packed Berry Smoothie

Total Calories Per Serving: 295

A perfect burst of sweetness with a potent punch of protein is sure to make breakfast a satisfying holdover to your next meal.

Makes 1 Smoothie

Ingredients
1 cup fresh spinach
1 small banana, sliced
4 ounces mixed berries
½ cup unsweetened almond milk
1 scoop whey protein

Directions
Step 1: Add all the ingredients together in a blender, starting with the spinach and ending with the almond milk and whey protein.
Step 2: Blend on high speed until smooth. Pour and serve.

Variation
If you want to pare down this smoothie, add only half a scoop of whey protein and save yourself about 60 calories. For a creamier smoothie, use unsweetened coconut milk instead of the almond, which will add on another 5 calories, which you can augment by eliminating the spinach.

Nutritional Information

	% Daily Value		
Calories 295		Total Carbohydrates 43.3 g	14%
Calories from Fat 42		Dietary Fiber 8 g	32%
		Sugars 23.9 g	
Total Fat 4.7 g	7%	Protein 24.2 g	
Saturated Fat 1.1 g	6%	Vitamin A	64%
Trans Fat 0		Vitamin C	70%
Cholesterol 50mg	17%	Calcium	38%
Sodium 235mg	10%	Iron	15%

Orange "Creamsicle" Smoothie

Total Calories Per Serving: 240

Who doesn't love a creamy orange popsicle on a hot summer after-noon? Well, why wait—for the summer or until after lunch? This delicious, fruity, and healthy "creamsicle in a cup" is a refreshing, satisfying way to start the day.

Makes 1 Smoothie

Ingredients

> 1 small banana, sliced
> 1¼ cups assorted berries
> ¼ cup low-fat plain yogurt
> 1 cup light orange juice

Directions

Step 1: Add the fruit, yogurt and juice to a blender.
Step 2: Blend on medium speed until smooth and creamy, about 2 minutes. Serve immediately.

Nutritional Information

Calories 240		Total Carbohydrates 55.4 g	18%
Calories from Fat 10		Dietary Fiber 7.6 g	31%
	% Daily Value	Sugars 37.7 g	
Total Fat 1.1 g	2%	Protein 5.8 g	
Saturated Fat 0.7 g	4%	Vitamin A	2%
Trans Fat 0		Vitamin C	315%
Cholesterol 4mg	1%	Calcium	14%
Sodium 54mg	2%	Iron	7%

Virgin Apple-tini Smoothie

Total Calories Per Serving: 265

Makes 1 Smoothie

Ingredients

1 cup Granny Smith apples, peeled, cored, and chopped
1 banana
½ cup light apple juice
¼ cup nonfat plain yogurt
Pinch of cinnamon or nutmeg, if desired

Directions

Step 1: Combine all ingredients in a blender. Blend until creamy and smooth, about a minute or two.

Step 2: Just for fun, pour into a martini glass, sprinkle with a a a pinch of cinnamon or nutmeg, if desired, and enjoy. (If you want to garnish with an apple slice, go ahead. That's only about 4 extra calories!)

Nutritional Information

Calories 265		Total Carbohydrates 60.9 g	20%
Calories from Fat 12		Dietary Fiber 5.9 g	23%
	% Daily Value	Sugars 43.7 g	
Total Fat 1.4 g	2%	Protein 4.9 g	
Saturated Fat 0.8 g	4%	Vitamin A	3%
Trans Fat 0		Vitamin C	112%
Cholesterol 4mg	1%	Calcium	13%
Sodium 49mg	2%	Iron	5%

Simple Strawberry-Banana Smoothie

Total Calories Per Serving: 201

A smoothie classic! The flavors of strawberries and bananas combine for a yummy, filling breakfast treat. Just a touch of honey gives it all the extra sweetness it needs.

Makes 2 Smoothies

Ingredients

   Approximately 15 strawberries, hulled
   1 medium banana, peeled and roughly chopped
   1 cup 1% low-fat milk
   ½ cup plain nonfat yogurt
   1 teaspoon honey

Directions

Step 1: Place all the above ingredients into a blender.
Step 2: Blend until smooth. Pour into glasses and enjoy.

Nutritional Information

Calories 201		Total Carbohydrates 36.1 g	12%
Calories from Fat 19		Dietary Fiber 3.2 g	13%
	% Daily Value	Sugars 27.5 g	
Total Fat 2.1 g	3%	Protein 9.1 g	
Saturated Fat 1.5 g	7%	Vitamin A	6%
Trans Fat 0		Vitamin C	145%
Cholesterol 10mg	3%	Calcium	28%
Sodium 97mg	4%	Iron	3%

Mulled Spice Banana Smoothie

Total Calories Per Serving: 199

The flavor of banana gets a special kick with the addition of mulling spices. This thick treat is sure to satisfy. If you find it to be too thick for your liking, add ¼ cup of water.

Makes 2 Smoothies

Ingredients

1 banana, peeled and broken into chunks
1 cup plain nonfat French vanilla yogurt
¾ teaspoon mulling spice (see below)

Directions

Step 1: Place banana chunks, yogurt, and mulling spice in a blender.
Step 2: Blend until smooth. Pour into glasses and serve immediately.

Mulling Spice

1 ½ cups brown sugar
¾ tablespoon ground cinnamon
½ tablespoon orange peel
½ tablespoon ground cloves
½ tablespoon ground allspice
¼ tablespoon ground nutmeg
Mix all together and store in an airtight container.

Nutritional Information

Calories 199		Total Carbohydrates 43.5 g	15%
Calories from Fat 13		Dietary Fiber 3.1 g	12%
	% Daily Value	Sugars 30.3 g	
Total Fat 1.4 g	2%	Protein 6 g	
Saturated Fat 0.8 g	4%	Vitamin A	13%
Trans Fat 0		Vitamin C	17%
Cholesterol 3mg	1%	Calcium	17%
Sodium 71mg	3%	Iron	2%

Chapter 2: Salads

Of course we all believe that there isn't anything as healthy as a salad! In part, that's true. But sometimes those things we add to our salads to make them more, well, *"interesting"* actually work against our best weight-loss intentions. Ever have a salad that was higher in calories than a cheeseburger? I bet you have.

You won't now. Once you start paying attention to how high things are in calories, you may opt to go without them on fast days. Even some of the healthiest foods. For example, avocados are among the best food for you. Rich in "good" fats and filled with nutrients, these luscious, creamy gems are loaded with calories—about 365 in a medium-sized avocado. For a low-calorie salad, you're actually better off adding three to four ounces of lean chicken breast or lean steak (about 200 calories each) than a whole avocado. Go easy. Same holds for chickpeas. A cup of "naked" chickpeas has an amazing 286 calories! So yes, foods like these are filling and tasty, just use sparingly.

Dressing is also a killer when it comes to calories that count—but don't have to. While I have sampled and included some delicious low-cal dressings in this chapter, remember that a little bit goes a long way. Take an old trick from Weight Watchers and keep your dressing on the side instead of pouring it all over your salad. When you take a bite of food on your fork, lightly dip into the dressing. You'll be eating considerably less that way. (And if for some reason you can't finish your salad, it will keep much longer without dressing.)

Spinach Salad with Chicken

Total Calories Per Serving: 276

The flavors of chicken and spinach sparkle to life in this delicious, fresh, and low-calorie version of a typical spinach salad. Use balsamic vinegar in place of red wine vinegar if you prefer. The calories will be the same.

Makes 4 Servings

Ingredients

1 teaspoon shallots, minced
1 tablespoon red wine vinegar
4 cups baby spinach, rinsed, stems removed
2 boneless cooked chicken breast halves, skinless

1 pint cherry tomatoes, quartered
4 strips turkey bacon, cooked crisp, drained, and crumbled
3 tablespoons olive oil

Directions

Step 1: Soak shallots in the red wine vinegar and set aside.

Step 2: Add spinach leaves to a large bowl. Slice the chicken breast into bite-sized pieces and place over spinach. Top the chicken and spinach with the tomatoes and the crumbled turkey bacon and toss all the ingredients together.

Step 3: In a separate bowl, whisk the olive oil into the red wine vinegar and shallot mixture.

Step 4: Divide salad into four bowls and drizzle on dressing or serve dressing on the side.

Nutritional Information

Calories 276		Total Carbohydrates 4.2 g	1%
Calories from Fat 127		Dietary Fiber 1.6mg	6%
	% Daily Value	Sugars 2.1 g	
Total Fat 14.1 g	22%	Protein 32.2 g	
Saturated Fat 2.3 g	12%	Vitamin A	57%
Cholesterol 83mg	28%	Vitamin C	40%
Sodium 211mg	9%	Calcium	4%
		Iron	16%

Grilled Chicken and Tomato Salad

Total Calories Per Serving: 162

Tomatoes come in so many flavors, shapes, and sizes, you could cook with these vitamin-packed gems for a week in a row and never get sick of them. Arugula's satisfyingly sharp bite makes a great foundation of flavor for this tasty, filling, and colorful salad.

Makes 4 Servings

Ingredients

6 ounces chicken breast, skinless and boneless

6 cups arugula

4 heirloom tomatoes, cut into quarters

¼ cup red onion, chopped

2 tablespoons olive oil

2 teaspoons red wine vinegar

1 clove garlic

Directions

Step 1: Heat a grill pan to medium. Grill chicken 6 minutes per side. Set aside to cool.

Step 2: In a large bowl, toss arugula with tomatoes and onion. Slice slightly cooled chicken into bite size pieces and toss into salad.

Step 3: Drizzle on dressing, toss lightly, and serve.

Nutritional Information

Calories 162		Total Carbohydrates 6 g	2%
Calories from Fat 83		Dietary Fiber 1.6 g	7%
	% Daily Value	Sugars 1.9 g	
Total Fat 9.2 g	14%	Protein 15.6 g	
Saturated Fat 1 g	5%	Vitamin A	14%
Trans Fat 0		Vitamin C	24%
Cholesterol 36mg	12%	Calcium	6%
Sodium 177mg	7%	Iron	8%

Goat Cheese with Fruit Salad

Total Calories Per Serving: 205

Here's a light, vitamin-packed salad that makes a flavorful lunch. The texture and flavor of the soft cheese actually negates having to add a dressing.

Makes 2 Servings

Ingredients

4 cups mixed baby greens
1 cup mandarin oranges
1 cup strawberries, sliced
2 cucumbers, sliced
1 cup grape tomatoes
1 cup mushrooms, sliced
2 ounces goat cheese, at room temperature
⅛ cup almond slivers

Directions

Step 1: Rinse and dry the salad greens and place in a large bowl. Add the mandarin oranges, the strawberry slices, the tomatoes, cucumber slices, and mushrooms and toss.

Step 2: Stir in the goat cheese and serve. Top each salad with a sprinkling of almonds and enjoy.

Nutritional Information

Calories 205		Total Carbohydrates 24.8 g	8%
Calories from Fat 78		Dietary Fiber 6 g	24%
	% Daily Value	Sugars 11.8 g	
Total Fat 8.7 g	13%	Protein 11.4 g	
Saturated Fat 3.8 g	19%	Vitamin A	59%
Trans Fat		Vitamin C	106%
Cholesterol 15mg	5%	Calcium	22%
Sodium 100mg	4%	Iron	17%

Asian-Inspired Fried Chicken Salad

Total Calories Per Serving: 264

You don't often hear the words "fried chicken" and "salad" together in a recipe, and yes, it's hard to believe that you can enjoy fried chicken on a diet. But as is the case with most foods, you can shave so much of the "bad" away by taking care in the way you prepare foods. Here, by eliminating the breading, you can still enjoy the flavor of fried chicken without the bulk, and you get to savor the crunch of fried chicken with the addition of peanuts.

Makes 4 Servings

Ingredients

1 pound chicken breast tenders
¼ cup fat-free, low-sodium chicken broth
2 tablespoons rice wine vinegar
1 tablespoon Thai fish sauce
1 tablespoon low-sodium soy sauce

1 tablespoon garlic, chopped
1 tablespoon peanut oil
4 cups mixed salad greens
¼ cup fresh basil, chopped
½ cup thinly sliced red onion
2 tablespoons finely chopped unsalted, dry-roasted peanuts

Directions

Step 1: In a medium to large sized bowl, whisk together the broth, rice wine vinegar, fish sauce, soy sauce, and garlic. Cover and marinate chicken for at least half an hour and as long as overnight.

Step 2: Heat peanut oil in a large nonstick skillet over medium-high heat. Add chicken to the pan and cook through, about 5-6 minutes per side. Add the remaining marinade and cook on low heat an additional 2-4 minutes as liquid thickens. Set aside.

Step 3: Toss salad greens, basil, and onion in a bowl and pour out onto a serving platter. Top with chicken, sprinkle with peanuts, and serve.

Nutritional Information

Calories 264		Total Carbohydrates 12 g	4%
Calories from Fat 99		Dietary Fiber 1.3 g	5%
	% Daily Value	Sugars 3.6 g	
Total Fat 11 g	17%	Protein 28.4 g	
Saturated Fat 1.3 g	7%	Vitamin A	33%
Trans Fat		Vitamin C	58%
Cholesterol 46mg	15%	Calcium	3%
Sodium 855mg	36%	Iron	7%

Leftover Turkey Salad

Total Calories Per Serving: 299

Here's a great way to use up that seemingly endless leftover turkey you get stuck with after hosting Thanksgiving! While it would not be advised to make this a Thanksgiving substitution meal (because that might be torturous), it's a great day-after "food hangover" remedy— and also a satisfying meal for any time of year.

Makes 4 servings

Ingredients

2 tablespoons olive oil
1 tablespoon cider vinegar
1 teaspoon dijon mustard
4 cups baby spinach
1 pound turkey breast, sliced
2 slices cooked turkey bacon, crumbled
1 cup avocado, sliced
8 cherry tomatoes, quartered

Directions

Step 1: In a bowl, whisk together the vinegar, mustard, and olive oil. Set aside.

Step 2: In another bowl, toss together the spinach, turkey, bacon, and tomatoes. Toss the salad with the dressing and plate. Lay the avocado slices on top and serve.

Nutritional Information

Calories 299		Total Carbohydrates 18.7 g	6%
Calories from Fat 136		Dietary Fiber 6.7 g	27%
	% Daily Value	Sugars 10.8 g	
Total Fat 15.1 g	23%	Protein 24.g	
Saturated Fat 2.2 g	11%	Vitamin A	59%
Trans Fat		Vitamin C	118%
Cholesterol 54mg	18%	Calcium	5%
Sodium 1264mg	53%	Iron	37%

Creamy Green Salad with "Presto" Pesto

Total Calories Per Serving: 214

Creamy avocado and luscious pesto are two great tastes that are amazing together, and don't pack on the pounds if you watch how you're using them. I've been making pesto from the recipe below for years and it's heavenly on pasta and salmon. But it also makes a wonderful salad dressing. Kalamata olives complete the effect, grounding the meal with a nice, salty kick!

Makes 2 Servings

Ingredients
    4 cups of mixed salad greens
    1 tablespoon pesto (see below)
    ½ avocado, cut into chunks
    10 kalamata olives, halved and pitted

Directions
Step 1: Place salad greens in a large bowl and lightly toss with pesto.
Step 2: Toss in avocado and olives; plate and serve.

Presto Pesto!
Calories per tablespoon: 76
    1 up fresh basil leaves, packed
    2 cloves garlic, minced
    ½ cup grated cheese
    ⅛ cup pine nuts
    1 cup olive oil

Add all ingredients less ½ cup olive oil to a food processor and pulse until chopped. Slowly add the rest of the olive oil while pulsing, until the texture appears smooth.

Nutritional Information

Calories 214		Total Carbohydrates 7.5 g	3%
Calories from Fat 59		Dietary Fiber 2.1 g	8%
	% Daily Value	Protein 2.7 g	
Total Fat 6.6 g	10%	Vitamin A	43%
Saturated Fat 1 g	5%	Vitamin C	58%
Trans Fat		Calcium	4%
Cholesterol 1mg	0%	Iron	8%
Sodium 158 mg	7%		

Hawaiian Mache Salad

Total Calories Per Serving: 218

Like a luau on a plate! This salad calls for mache, which is a soft, sweet, nutty leaf and a nice compliment to the saltiness of the ham and sweetness of the pineapple.

Makes 2 servings

Ingredients

  2 cups fresh pineapple, cubed
  2 tablespoons chopped fresh cilantro
  2 tablespoons fresh orange juice
  4 teaspoons apple cider vinegar
  1 large garlic clove
  ¼ cup extra-virgin olive oil
  4 cups mache lettuce
  ⅔ cup thinly sliced red bell pepper
  ½ cup thinly sliced red onion
  1 cup ham, cubed

Directions

Step 1: In a blender or food processor, add 1 cup of the pineapple with the orange juice, vinegar, garlic, and olive oil. Pulse until smooth and set aside.

Step 2: In a large bowl, toss mache with the chunks of ham, remaining pineapple, red bell pepper, and onion. Drizzle with dressing and chopped cilantro and toss. Plate and serve.

Nutritional Information

Calories 218		Total Carbohydrates 15.8 g	5%
Calories from Fat 141		Dietary Fiber 2.5 g	10%
	% Daily Value	Sugars 9.5 g	
Total Fat 15.7 g	24%	Protein 7.1 g	
Saturated Fat 2.8 g	14%	Vitamin A	38%
Trans Fat		Vitamin C	114%
Cholesterol 19mg	6%	Calcium	5%
Sodium 459mg	19%	Iron	5%

Spicy Pork Salad

Total Calories Per Serving: 260

In small doses, pork doesn't have to be on your "do not eat" list if you're trying to lose weight. A four-ounce portion of trimmed, lean tenderloin is about 122 calories. Pair that with a large portion of healthy greens and other veggies and you get a satisfying, healthy alternative way to enjoy pork. Turn down the "heat" by scaling down the hot sauce or eliminating it altogether.

Makes 4 Servings

Ingredients

12 ounces pork tenderloin, trimmed
1 tablespoon hot sauce
2 tablespoons brown sugar
½ teaspoon garlic powder
¼ teaspoon salt
Cooking spray

3 cups baby spinach leaves
1 cup peppers (red, yellow, and orange peppers), roughly chopped
⅛ cup low-fat sesame ginger dressing

Directions

Step 1: Slice raw tenderloin crosswise into ½-inch slices.

Step 2: In a bowl, lightly mix hot sauce with brown sugar, garlic powder, and salt. Toss pork slices in mixture and set aside.

Step 3: Coat a large nonstick skillet and heat at medium-high heat. Once the pan is hot, add pork and cook 3 minutes on each side. Remove from heat; keep warm.

Step 4: Toss spinach with peppers and dressing. Plate and top each salad with the spicy pork.

Nutritional Information

Calories 260		Total Carbohydrates 13 g	4%
Calories from Fat 35		Dietary Fiber 3.1 g	12%
	% Daily Value	Sugars 5.7 g	
Total Fat 3.9 g	6%	Protein 24 g	
Saturated Fat 1.1 g	6%	Vitamin A	43%
Trans Fat		Vitamin C	18%
Cholesterol 62 mg	21%	Calcium	7%
Sodium 397 mg	17%	Iron	25%

Island Madness Fruity Pork Salad

Total Calories Per Serving: 294

Pork tenderloin, spiced up with a touch of cumin, transforms a sweet spinach and tropical fruit salad into a satisfying full meal.

Makes 2 servings

Ingredients

2 teaspoons ground cumin

1 cup chicken broth

6 ounces pork tenderloin, cut into strips

1 tablespoon cornstarch

4 cups baby spinach

½ cup papaya, cut into chunks

½ cup mango, cut into chunks

2 tablespoons chopped fresh cilantro

1 tablespoon lime juice

1 tablespoon honey

¼ teaspoon freshly ground black pepper

⅛ teaspoon crushed red-pepper flakes

Directions

Step 1: Heat a large skillet over medium and add the cumin, stirring frequently until fragrant. Set aside half the cumin on a nearby dish and leave the other half in the skillet.

Step 2: Turn up heat to high and add broth to the skillet. Bring to a boil.

Step 3: Once the broth is boiling, add the pork and reduce the heat to medium. Cover and cook, stirring occasionally, until the pork is no longer pink, about 4 minutes. Then remove the pork and toss it with the additional cumin.

Step 4: Bring heat to high and boil until the liquid is reduced to about ¼ cup. Whisk in the cornstarch until the liquid becomes thick and remove from the heat.

Step 5: Place spinach leaves and fruit chunks in a large bowl and set aside.

Step 6: In another bowl, combine the cilantro, lime juice, honey, crushed red-pepper flakes, and black pepper, and whisk in the thickened liquid.

Step 7: Add the cooled pork to the spinach and fruit. Toss with dressing and serve.

Nutritional Information

Calories 294		Total Carbohydrates 37.7 g	13%
Calories from Fat 45		Dietary Fiber 4.4 g	17%
	% Daily Value	Sugars 27 g	
Total Fat 5 g	8%	Protein 27.6 g	
Saturated Fat 1.4 g	7%	Vitamin A	138%
Trans Fat		Vitamin C	117%
Cholesterol 62mg	21%	Calcium	11%
Sodium 486mg	20%	Iron	25%

Sumptuous Steak Salad

Total Calories Per Serving: 271

If you have a taste for red meat, here's a gorgeous way to savor the flavor without sacrificing your health. The mustardy-sharpness of arugula is a great base for a small portion of steak—just enough to satisfy the craving. The pine nuts lend extra crunch and the shaved parmesan cheese makes it savory. (Though you could lessen the calorie count if you eliminated one of these indulgences.)

Makes 2 servings

Ingredients

¼ teaspoon salt
½ teaspoon black pepper
1 4-ounce flat iron steak
1 tablespoon extra-virgin olive oil
1 tablespoon fresh lemon juice
½ teaspoon dijon mustard
4 cups arugula

1 cup cherry tomatoes, quartered
1 cucumber, peeled and sliced
1 cup mushrooms, sliced
2 teaspoons pine nuts
1 ounce solid parmesan cheese, shaved

Directions

Step 1: Fire up your grill to high or heat a grill pan over medium-high heat. While grill or grill pan is heating, rub steak with pepper and salt.

Step 2: Add steak to pan; cook 4 minutes on each side for medium rare. Remove and set aside 10 minutes to rest.

Step 3: Place the arugula on a serving platter and top with veggies. Slice the steak into strips and add the strips to the salad.

Step 4: In a small bowl, whisk together olive oil, lemon juice, and mustard, and drizzle over salad. Sprinkle with pine nuts and shaved parmesan cheese and serve.

Nutritional Information

Calories 271		Total Carbohydrates 12.4 g	4%
Calories from Fat 149		Dietary Fiber 3 g	12%
	% Daily Value	Sugars 6.1 g	
Total Fat 16.6 g	26%	Protein 20.7 g	
Saturated Fat 5 g	25%	Vitamin A	24%
Trans Fat		Vitamin C	51%
Cholesterol 35 mg	12%	Calcium	27%
Sodium 751 mg	31%	Iron	25%

Asian-Inspired Steak Salad

Total Calories Per Serving: 244

Sugar and spice and everything nice. . . . Here's a "hot" Asian-inspired steak salad that will fill your tummy (and probably clear your sinuses at the same time). If you prefer a little less heat, cut down the chili paste, or cut it out altogether. It will still be delicious—and the juices from the steak will be the only dressing you'll need.

Makes 4 servings

Ingredients

½ cup fresh lime juice
¼ cup chopped fresh cilantro
2 tablespoons brown sugar
2 tablespoons Thai fish sauce
1 tablespoon chili paste
2 garlic cloves, minced

1 8 ounce flank steak, trimmed
4-6 large handfuls mixed salad
greens
½ pint grape tomatoes, halved
1 tablespoon toasted sesame
seeds

Directions

Step 1: Combine lime juice, cilantro, brown sugar, fish sauce, chili paste, and garlic in a bowl and whisk together. Pour over steak and marinate for at least half an hour and as long as overnight. (Don't refrigerate if grilling within 2 hours.)

Step 2: If steak has been refrigerated, remove at least an hour before cooking to bring meat close to room temperature. Heat grill or grill pan and spray with cooking spray.

Step 3: Grill steak 5 minutes per side for medium rare, 7 per side for well done. Remove from heat and allow steak to rest 10 minutes.

Step 4: While steak is resting, toss salad greens with tomatoes and plate on a serving platter.

Step 5: Slice steak thinly and plate over the greens and tomatoes. Sprinkle with toasted sesame seeds and serve while the steak is still warm.

Nutritional Information

Calories 244		Total Carbohydrates 24.7 g	8%
Calories from Fat 64		Dietary Fiber 7.4 g	30%
	% Daily Value	Sugars 6.3 g	
Total Fat 7.1 g	11%	Protein 23.5 g	
Saturated Fat 2.2 g	11%	Vitamin A	82%
Trans Fat		Vitamin C	50%
Cholesterol 31mg	10%	Calcium	13%
Sodium 883mg	37%	Iron	20%

Pomegranate-Power Steak Salad

Total Calories Per Serving: 282

Pomegranates are delicious and they've become especially popular in recent years for their amazing healthful qualities. They're good for your heart, good for your brain, and a great source of vitamins C and K, fiber, and folate. Combine pomegranate with other power foods like almonds and spinach, and you've got a salad that packs a punch! (Of nutrients, that is.)

Makes 4 Servings

Ingredients

Cooking spray

12 ounces hanger steak

¼ cup 100% pomegranate juice

Splash of white wine vinegar

1 tablespoon dijon mustard

4 teaspoons extra-virgin olive oil

1 teaspoon honey

1 12-ounce package of baby spinach

1 cup mandarin orange slices

½ cup pomegranate seeds

¼ cup roasted, unsalted almonds

salt and freshly ground black pepper

Directions

Step 1: Heat a grill pan on medium or fire up your grill. Coat with cooking spray.

Step 2: While the pan or grill warms, combine the juice with the vinegar, mustard, olive oil, and honey in a small bowl and set aside.

Step 3: Cook the steak to your preference, 5 minutes per side for medium rare, and 7 per side for medium well.

Step 4: While the steak cools, toss the spinach, oranges, and pomegranate seeds with the dressing in a bowl, and plate on a large platter.

Step 5: Slice the steak thinly and place the slices on top of the salad. Top with almonds, season with salt and pepper, and serve.

Nutritional Information

Calories 282		Total Carbohydrates 28.2 g	9%
Calories from Fat 129		Dietary Fiber 4 g	16%
	% Daily Value	Sugars 19.8 g	
Total Fat 14.3 g	22%	Protein 26.5 g	
Saturated Fat 2.8 g	14%	Vitamin A	160%
Trans Fat		Vitamin C	51%
Cholesterol 63mg	21%	Calcium	12%
Sodium 201mg	8%	Iron	95%

Jamaican Jerk-Rubbed Scallop Salad

Total Calories Per Serving: 195

Did you know that scallops are one of the lowest-calorie sources of protein available? It's true! A 3-ounce serving of scallops, plainly prepared, is just about 75 calories. (Compare that to skinless chicken breast at 110 calories, salmon at 128 calories, or mussels at 147 calories!) This recipe weds this mighty shellfish with flavors of the Caribbean, making it taste like summer any time of year!

Makes 4 servings

Ingredients
1 tablespoon Jamaican jerk rub (see below)
12 large sea scallops
Cooking spray
4 large handfuls of gourmet salad greens
⅓ cup fresh pineapple, chunked
⅓ cup mango chunks
⅓ cup avocado chunks
2 tablespoons fresh lime juice
2 teaspoons olive oil

Directions
Step 1: Prepare Jamaican jerk rub (using recipe below) or use prepared rub.
Step 2: Rinse and pat dry scallops, and lightly dredge each scallop in the rub. Set aside.
Step 3: Heat grill pan and coat with cooking spray. Place scallops in pan and grill 3 minutes per side. Remove from pan and set aside to cool slightly.
Step 4: In a large bowl, toss together salad greens, pineapple, avocado, and mango.
Step 5: In a separate small bowl, whisk together olive oil and lime juice, and toss it into the salad and fruits.
Step 6: Plate the salad on a serving platter. Top with scallops and serve.

Continued . . .

Jamaican Jerk Rub

½ teaspoon ground allspice

½ teaspoon dried thyme

⅓ teaspoon curry powder

½ teaspoon paprika

⅓ teaspoon sugar

¼ teaspoon salt

¼ teaspoon black pepper

½ teaspoon cayenne pepper

⅛ teaspoon grated nutmeg

⅛ teaspoon ground cinnamon

¹⁄₁₆ teaspoon ground cloves

Toss ingredients together and use on seafood, chicken, meat, and more.

Nutritional Information

Calories 195		Total Carbohydrates 5.5 g	6%
Calories from Fat 45		Dietary Fiber 1 g	4%
	% Daily Value	Sugars 1.5 g	
Total Fat 5 g	8%	Protein 15.4 g	
Saturated Fat .07 g	3%	Vitamin A	1%
Trans Fat		Vitamin C	21%
Cholesterol 30mg	10%	Calcium	3%
Sodium 146mg	6%	Iron	2%

Bacon & Shrimp Salad

Total Calories Per Serving: 190

Turkey bacon is a miracle! No, it doesn't have the "full impact" of regular bacon, but that goes both ways. At just 30 calories per slice of turkey bacon—how can you go wrong? Here's a tasty way to use it in a simple recipe low in fat and calories and high in flavor!

Makes 4 servings

Ingredients

2 slices turkey bacon

1½ pounds large shrimp, peeled and deveined

5 cups arugula leaves

1 cup cherry tomatoes, halved

1 teaspoon balsamic vinegar

1 tablespoon extra virgin olive oil

¼ teaspoon black pepper

Directions

Step 1: Heat a nonstick skillet over medium heat and cook bacon until crisp. Remove, drain, and set aside to cool.

Step 2: In the same pan, and using the bacon drippings, cook shrimp, about 3 minutes per side.

Step 3: In a large bowl, toss together arugula leaves, halved cherry tomatoes, and shrimp.

Step 4: In a small bowl, whisk together balsamic vinegar, oil, and pepper. Drizzle over other ingredients and toss gently to combine.

Step 5: Divide among 4 plates, top with turkey bacon, and serve.

Nutritional Information

Calories 190		Total Carbohydrates 5.5 g	2%
Calories from Fat 36		Dietary Fiber	4%
	% Daily Value	Sugars	
Total Fat 4 g	6%	Protein	
Saturated Fat .05 g	3%	Vitamin A	12%
Trans Fat		Vitamin C	19%
Cholesterol 248mg	83%	Calcium	4%
Sodium 281mg	12%	Iron	6%

Grilled Shrimp & Corn Salad

Total Calories Per Serving: 261

Crackling with flavor, a salad with shrimp and sweet corn is like summer on a plate. A "creamy" dressing is made without using a drop of cream. Just luscious avocado, bursting with good fats and nutrients. In the interest of speed, this recipes calls for cooking frozen corn, but you can also grill or boil whole ears of fresh corn and remove from cob.

Makes 4 Servings

Ingredients

½ ripe avocado, pitted and peeled
3 tablespoons lime juice
⅛ cup to ¼ cup water (optional)
1 tablespoon chopped fresh basil
ground black pepper

Cooking spray
1 pound medium shrimp, peeled and deveined
salt and ground black pepper
1 package of frozen corn
6 cups mixed salad greens
2 plum tomatoes, chopped

Directions

Step 1: Add avocado, lime juice, basil, and pepper to a blender or food processor. Blend until smooth. If you wish to thin the consistency, pour in water, a small amount at a time, and pulse. Set dressing aside.

Step 2: Heat a grill pan on medium and coat with cooking spray. Season shrimp with salt and pepper and cook about 2-3 minutes per side. Transfer to a bowl, but leave drippings.

Step 3: Cook corn according to package directions and drain. Toss corn in pan drippings and remove with slotted spoon.

Step 4: In a large bowl, toss corn and shrimp with salad greens, tomatoes, and dressing. Serve immediately.

Nutritional Information

Calories 261		Total Carbohydrates 20.4 g	7%
Calories from Fat 51		Dietary Fiber 3.3 g	14%
	% Daily Value	Sugars 4 g	
Total Fat 5.7 g	9%	Protein 29.2 g	
Saturated Fat 0.6 g	3%	Vitamin A	57%
Trans Fat		Vitamin C	118%
Cholesterol 223mg	74%	Calcium	7%
Sodium 321mg	13%	Iron	36%

"California Roll" Crab and Avocado Salad

Total Calories Per Serving: 289

Well, maybe not a California Roll per se, as there's no rice or seaweed to be found here, but the other ingredients, topped with the popular carrot-ginger dressing served in Japanese restaurants, will definitely bring that popular sushi snack to mind!

Makes 4 Servings

Ingredients

- 2 large carrots, peeled and chopped
- 1 tablespoon fresh ginger
- 2 tablespoons sesame oil
- 2 tablespoons rice wine vinegar
- ¼ to ½ cup water (optional)
- 4 large handfuls mesclun greens
- 1 pound cooked lump crab meat
- 1 avocado, pitted, peeled and sliced
- 1 cucumber, diced
- 1 tablespoon toasted sesame seeds

Directions

Step 1: Add carrots, ginger, sesame oil, and rice vinegar to a blender or food processor. Blend until smooth. If dressing needs to be thinned, add water a small amount at a time and pulse until you get to your desired consistency.

Step 2: Lay greens down on a serving platter. Top with crab, avocado, and cucumber and drizzle on dressing. (Reserve excess, if desired.) Sprinkle with sesame seeds and serve.

Nutritional Information

Calories 289		Total Carbohydrates 17.3mg	6%
Calories from Fat 222		Dietary Fiber 6.7 g	27%
	% Daily Value	Sugars 3.4 g	
Total Fat 24.7 g	38%	Protein 20.3 g	
Saturated Fat 2.3 g	11%	Vitamin A	143%
Trans Fat		Vitamin C	21%
Cholesterol 64mg	21%	Calcium	44%
Sodium 691mg	29%	Iron	15%

Asian-Inspired Quinoa Salad

Total Calories Per Serving: 124

Holy quinoa, the miracle grain. While calorie-counters sometimes veer away from this calorie-packed grain, the benefits well outweigh this, and, used in wise amounts, quinoa satisfies on so many levels. Combined with the ingredients in this salad, quinoa gets an Asian-inspired spin. Though truly, this versatile grain can be "spun" in so many ways.

Makes 4 Servings

Ingredients

½ cup quinoa
⅓ cup diced red bell pepper
½ cup scallions, thinly sliced
½ cup cucumber, diced
3 tablespoons fresh lime juice
1 tablespoon olive oil

1 teaspoon light agave nectar
¼ teaspoon fine sea salt
¼ teaspoon ground black pepper
1 teaspoon toasted sesame seeds

Directions

Step 1: Prepare quinoa according to package directions.
Step 2: Add cooked quinoa to a bowl and fold in the bell pepper, scallions, and cucumber. Toss to combine.
Step 3: In a separate bowl, whisk together the lime juice, olive oil, agave, toasted sesame seeds, salt, and black pepper. Toss into quinoa mixture and serve.

Nutritional Information

	% Daily Value			
Calories 124		Total Carbohydrates 17.2 g	6%
Calories from Fat 46		Dietary Fiber 2.1 g	8%
		Sugars 2.4 g	
Total Fat 5.1 g	8%	Protein 3.4 g	
Saturated Fat 0.7 g	3%	Vitamin A	8%
Trans Fat		Vitamin C	27%
Cholesterol	0%	Calcium	3%
Sodium 4mg	0%	Iron	7%

Tex-Mex Quinoa Toss

Total Calories Per Serving: 281

Here's another yummy and exciting way to make a salad using quinoa as the main ingredient. Feel like a little Tex-Mex for dinner?
Serve this Tex-Mex-light toss and enjoy the wonderful flavor without
the worry!

Makes 6 Servings

Ingredients

⅛ cup fresh lemon juice
¼ cup olive oil
3 tbsp chopped fresh cilantro
Sea salt and fresh ground black
    pepper, to taste
½ cup quinoa
Pinch of ground cumin
1 cup cooked black beans,
    drained

1 plum tomato, diced
1 cup corn
1 zucchini, diced
1 yellow squash, diced
2 bell peppers (red, yellow, or
    orange), diced
¼ cup red onion, chopped

Directions

Step 1: Cook quinoa according to package directions. Remove from
        heat, fluff with fork, and let sit to cool slightly.
Step 2: In a large bowl, whisk together lemon juice, olive oil, cilantro,
        cumin, salt, and pepper, and fold cooled quinoa into dressing.
Step 3: Add beans, tomato, and vegetables and gently stir until ingre-
        dients are evenly mixed. Serve immediately or refrigerate and
        serve chilled.

Nutritional Information

Calories 281		Total Carbohydrates 39.3 g	13%
Calories from Fat 91		Dietary Fiber 8.3 g	33%
	% Daily Value	Sugars 4.6 g	
Total Fat 10.1 g	16%	Protein 10.8 g	
Saturated Fat 1.5 g	8%	Vitamin A	28%
Trans Fat		Vitamin C	110%
Cholesterol	0%	Calcium	6%
Sodium 12mg	1%	Iron	19%

Warm Lemony-Pepper Orzo Salad

Total Calories Per Serving: 249

Orzo makes a nice alternative to a pasta for making a pasta salad. It's about as intrusive as rice, which means it allows the ingredients added to it to really pop—in this case, a lovely combination of lemon, garlic, and bell peppers.

Makes 4 servings

Ingredients

1 cup orzo
¼ teaspoon grated lemon rind
3 tablespoons fresh lemon juice
1 tablespoon extra-virgin olive oil
½ teaspoon minced garlic
½ teaspoon kosher salt
⅛ teaspoon freshly ground black pepper
½ cup red bell pepper, chopped
½ cup yellow bell pepper, chopped
½ cup feta cheese, crumbled

Directions

Step 1: Cook orzo according to package directions.

Step 2: While orzo cooks, whisk together lemon rind, lemon juice, olive oil, garlic, salt and pepper in a medium sized to large bowl.

Step 3: When orzo finishes cooking, drain and rinse with cold water and add to bowl with dressing. Gently fold the orzo into the dressing.

Step 4: Stir in the bell peppers and feta cheese. Serve immediately, at room temperature, or cover and refrigerate for 2 hours to serve chilled.

Nutritional Information

Calories 249		Total Carbohydrates 34.4 g	11%
Calories from Fat 76		Dietary Fiber 2.1 g	8%
	% Daily Value	Sugars 4.3 g	
Total Fat 8.4 g	13%	Protein 8.3 g	
Saturated Fat 3.4 g	17%	Vitamin A	16%
Trans Fat		Vitamin C	58%
Cholesterol 17mg	6%	Calcium	10%
Sodium 503mg	21%	Iron	9%

Green Apple and Gorgonzola Salad

Total Calories Per Serving: 282

One of my favorite taste combinations is green apples and gorgonzola. I could slather slices of green apple with gorgonzola and eat them like potato chips. If this is also one of your favorite combinations, this simple salad is sure to be a treat. You could omit the walnuts if you want to bank those calories, though at less than 300 calories with the walnuts, I don't see why you would!

Makes 4 servings

Ingredients

¼ cup olive oil

2 tablespoons red wine vinegar

1 teaspoon Dijon mustard

1 clove garlic, finely chopped

6 large handfuls of salad greens

1 green apple, peeled and chopped

½ cup crumbled gorgonzola cheese

⅓ cup chopped walnuts

Directions

Step 1: In a medium to large sized bowl, whisk together olive oil, vinegar, mustard, and garlic.

Step 2: Add salad greens, apples, cheese, and walnuts and fold together. Serve immediately.

Nutritional Information

Calories 282		Total Carbohydrates 10.7 g	4%
Calories from Fat 223		Dietary Fiber 3.3 g	13%
	% Daily Value	Sugars 4.9 g	
Total Fat 24.8	38%	Protein 8 g	
Saturated Fat 6.1 g	31%	Vitamin A	16%
Trans Fat		Vitamin C	7%
Cholesterol 20mg	7%	Calcium	12%
Sodium 292mg	12%	Iron	3%

Arugula with Fennel, Clementines, and Pecans

Total Calories Per Serving: 214

The wonderful, mustardy bite of arugula beautifully grounds sweeter salad ingredients—and makes it a perfect foil for the oranges in this crunchy, nutty salad, while the flavor of fennel carries this dish from "good" to "delish"!

Makes 4 Servings

Ingredients

3 tablespoons olive oil

1 tablespoon white wine vinegar

2 medium fennel bulbs, halved and sliced thin

3 small clementines, peeled and broken into wedges

1 small red onion, sliced thin, in rings

2 cups baby arugula leaves

¼ cup pecans

Directions

Step 1: In a medium bowl, whisk together the olive oil and the vinegar.

Step 2: In another bowl, toss together fennel, clementine wedges, and onion in large bowl. Fold in dressing and toss.

Step 3: Plate arugula leaves on a serving platter. Pour mixture on top of arugula leaves. Sprinkle with pecans and serve.

Nutritional Information

Calories 214		Total Carbohydrates 19 g	6%
Calories from Fat 137		Dietary Fiber 5.4 g	22%
	% Daily Value	Sugars 7.1 g	
Total Fat 15.3 g	23%	Protein 4 g	
Saturated Fat 2.1 g	10%	Vitamin A	24%
Trans Fat		Vitamin C	67%
Cholesterol	0%	Calcium	11%
Sodium 128mg	5%	Iron	9%

Sweet and Creamy Fennel Salad

Total Calories Per Serving: 258

Here's another wonderful way to pair orange and fennel—this time with creamy avocado in a lettuce-free salad.

Makes 2 Servings

Ingredients
1 fennel bulb
1 medium avocado, peeled, cored, and cubed
1 large navel orange, peeled and broken into wedges
1 tablespoon extra virgin olive oil
1 teaspoon cider vinegar
Salt and pepper, to taste

Directions
Step 1: Halve the fennel bulb and thinly slice those halves into slivers. Place in a medium bowl.

Step 2: Add the avocado and the orange wedges to the fennel and toss to combine.

Step 3: Whisk together the olive oil, vinegar, salt, and pepper in a small bowl, and drizzle the dressing over the salad. Serve immediately.

Nutritional Information

Calories 258		Total Carbohydrates 28 g	9%
Calories from Fat 199		Dietary Fiber 12.6 g	50%
	% Daily Value	Sugars 9.3 g	
Total Fat 22.1 g	34%	Protein 4.3 g	
Saturated Fat 3.1 g	16%	Vitamin A	10%
Trans Fat		Vitamin C	122%
Cholesterol		Calcium	11%
Sodium 68mg	3%	Iron	8%

Red Grapefruit, Mango, and Avocado Salad

Total Calories Per Serving: 288

The bittersweet sharpness of grapefruit nicely balances the sweetness of the mango and creaminess of the avocado here.

Makes 2 Servings

Ingredients
4 cups mixed baby greens
1 large ruby red grapefruit, peeled and sliced into sections
1 medium avocado, peeled, cored, and sliced
1 ripe mango, peeled, pitted, and sliced
2 tablespoons chopped red onion
2 teaspoons medium-dry sherry
1 tablespoon olive oil

Directions
Step 1: In a small bowl, soak the onion in the sherry and set aside.
Step 2: In a large bowl, toss together grapefruit, avocado, mango, and salad greens.
Step 3: Whisk the olive oil into the sherry-onion mixture. Pour over the salad and lightly toss. Serve immediately.

Nutritional Information

Calories 288		Total Carbohydrates 33.7 g	11%
Calories from Fat 201		Dietary Fiber 9.9 g	40%
	% Daily Value	Sugars 20.8 g	
Total Fat 22.3 g	34%	Protein 3.1 g	
Saturated Fat 3.2 g	16%	Vitamin A	19%
Trans Fat		Vitamin C	120%
Cholesterol	0%	Calcium	2%
Sodium 9mg	0%	Iron	6%

Asian Tofu Salad

Total Calories Per Serving: 239

Confession time: I never liked tofu before I started this diet, and that's because whenever I had it, it was always served chunked on top of other ingredients, with no thought ever given to sprucing it up a bit. Thanks to my research for this book, I've found lots of great ways to try tofu, and I really enjoy it now. Cooking the tofu in all of these rich, Asian-inspired flavors makes all the difference in this otherwise simple salad. There are plenty more tofu recipes included in the Vegetarian chapter for you to make and enjoy!

Makes 4 Servings

Ingredients

3 tablespoons canola oil

2 tablespoons rice vinegar

1 tablespoon honey

2 teaspoons reduced-sodium soy sauce

1 teaspoon toasted sesame oil

1 teaspoon minced fresh ginger

½ teaspoon salt

14 ounces extra-firm tofu, cubed

8 cups mixed salad greens

2 medium carrots, peeled, halved lengthwise and sliced

1 large cucumber, chopped

Directions

Step 1: Whisk the canola oil, vinegar, honey, soy sauce, sesame oil, ginger, and salt together in a bowl. Place 2 tablespoons of the dressing in a large nonstick skillet and heat over medium-high heat.

Step 2: When the skillet is hot, add cubes of tofu and cook 12-15 minutes, turning every 3 or so minutes.

Step 3: While the tofu is cooking, toss the greens, carrots, and cucumber with the remaining dressing. Plate on a serving platter and top with warm tofu. Serve immediately.

Nutritional Information

Calories 239		Total Carbohydrates 10.6 g	4%
Calories from Fat 53		Dietary Fiber 2.6 g	10%
	% Daily Value	Sugars 3.2 g	
Total Fat 5.9 g	9%	Protein 11.6 g	
Saturated Fat 0.6 g	3%	Vitamin A	233%
Trans Fat		Vitamin C	57%
Cholesterol	0%	Calcium	26%
Sodium 96mg	4%	Iron	27%

Chapter 3: Soups

Soups are a great way to fill up without eating heavily. Though like salads, soups can also harbor lots of hidden threats when it comes to calories.

One of the biggest culprits? Beans. Add a smattering of these little legumes to a soup and you'll be safe, but if you're being calorie-conscious, it's best to avoid them, no matter how nutritious they are in so many other ways. Save the beans for non-fast days!

Great ideas for soups are ones that are packed with **vegetables**. Add extra veggies to any of the soups with vegetables in this chapter and you'll amp up your satisfaction, making soup into stew, without adding calories or fat. Just be slightly wary: Not all vegetables are equal. Use the following chart to help you make smart choices.

Eat Smart!

Vegetable	Calories
Artichoke (1)	67
Asparagus (10 ounces)	54
Beets (8 ounces)	54
Bok choy (8 ounces)	29
Broccoli (8 ounces)	40
Brussels sprouts (8 ounces)	56
Cabbage (8 ounces)	31
Carrots (8 ounces)	45
Cauliflower (8 ounces)	31
Celery (3 stalks)	9
Corn (8 ounces)	140
Cucumber (1)	30
Eggplant (8 ounces)	38
Green beans (8 ounces)	31
Kale (8 ounces)	40
Mushrooms (8 ounces)	20
Onion (8 ounces)	65
Peas (8 ounces)	115
Peppers (8 ounces)	35
Pumpkin (8 ounces)	59
Mixed greens (8 ounces)	39
Radish (8 ounces)	20
Spinach (8 ounces)	14
Sweet potato (8 ounces)	172
Squash (8 ounces)	30
Turnip (8 ounces)	29
White potato (8 ounces)	146
Zucchini (8 ounces)	22

Yellow Split Pea Soup

Total Calories Per Serving: 248

Here's a bright and tasty variation on traditional green split pea soup. If you prefer a soup with a thicker consistency, be sure to mash the peas while they're cooking.

Makes 6 Servings

Ingredients

6-8 cups of vegetable broth
2 cups dry yellow split peas, rinsed
2 large carrots, chopped
1 sweet onion, chopped
6 cloves garlic, chopped
Salt and pepper, to taste

Directions

Step 1: Add the broth to a large stock pot and bring to a boil.

Step 2: Once the broth is boiling, add the split peas, carrots, garlic, and onions. Once the pot comes back to the boiling point, reduce heat to simmer and cover.

Step 3: Simmer about 45 minutes and check consistency. If too thick, add warm water; if too thin, consider mashing up the ingredients.

Step 4: Simmer an additional 15 to 20 minutes. Add salt and pepper to taste. Serve and enjoy.

Nutritional Information

Calories 186		Total Carbohydrates 44.9 g	15%
Calories from Fat 9		Dietary Fiber 17.9 g	71%
	% Daily Value	Sugars 7.3 g	
Total Fat 1 g	1%	Protein 16.9 g	
Saturated Fat		Vitamin A	82%
Trans Fat		Vitamin C	9%
Cholesterol	0%	Calcium	17%
Sodium 238mg	10%	Iron	17%

Creamy Cremini Soup

Total Calories Per Serving: 171

Few things are as perfect together as mushrooms and sour cream, and reduced-fat sour cream makes it possible to enjoy this fantastic flavor combination in this yummy soup recipe—less than 200 calories! Add a little lemon juice and white wine, and you've got heaven in a bowl.

Makes 6 servings

Ingredients

1½ teaspoons extra-virgin olive oil
1 large sweet onion, chopped
1 clove garlic, minced
1 pound cremini mushrooms, sliced
½ teaspoon dried thyme
½ cup white wine or dry vermouth
The juice of 1 lemon
3 tablespoons all-purpose flour
1 tablespoon butter
3 cups reduced-sodium chicken broth
1 cup reduced-fat sour cream
1 cup low-fat milk
Salt and pepper, to taste
Fresh parsley, chopped (optional)

Directions

Step 1: In a large stock pot or dutch oven, heat the olive oil on high until it's just smoking, then reduce heat to medium.

Step 2: Add the onions and sauté until soft, about 8 minutes. Add the garlic and continue to sauté and additional 2 minutes.

Step 3: Toss in the mushrooms with the onion and garlic and cook an additional 5-7 minutes—until the mushrooms brown slightly and lose their water. While the mushrooms are cooking, mash the flour and butter together to create a paste.

Step 4: Add the wine or vermouth and lemon juice and cook until liquid reduces by about ¼th—about 3 minutes. Stir in the flour paste until the mixture thickens.

Step 5: Add the broth and bring to a boil. Reduce heat to simmer. Whisk in the sour cream and milk. Simmer, covered, for 30 minutes.

Step 6: Remove from heat and ladle into bowls. Sprinkle with fresh parsley, if desired.

Nutritional Information

Calories 171		Total Carbohydrates 12.4 g	4%
Calories from Fat 93		Dietary Fiber 2.1 g	8%
	% Daily Value	Sugars 4.9 g	
Total Fat 10.4 g	16%	Protein 7.6 g	
Saturated Fat 5.8 g	29%	Vitamin A	5%
Trans Fat		Vitamin C	4%
Cholesterol 20mg	7%	Calcium	6%
Sodium 458mg	19%	Iron	4%

Classic Cabbage Soup

Total Calories Per Serving: 185

If this isn't your first diet, it's pretty certain you've either heard of or had some experience experimenting with the Cabbage Soup Diet. If you haven't, it's essentially a strict, seven-day regimen you can only do a week at a time. Cabbage soup is yummy, though, and you can enjoy it on any diet. Here's a tasty version that hits well under the 300-calorie mark!

Makes 6 Servings

Ingredients

1 tablespoon extra virgin olive oil

1 large sweet onion, chopped

5 cloves garlic

2 cups chopped bell pepper

4 cups chopped carrots

2 cups chopped celery

4 cups mushrooms, sliced

6 cups chicken broth

1 head cabbage, chopped

Water

Directions

Step 1: In a large stock pot or dutch oven, heat the olive oil on high until it's just smoking, then reduce heat to medium.

Step 2: Add the onions and sauté until soft, about 8 minutes. Add the garlic and continue to sauté an additional 2 minutes. Next, toss in the peppers and heat until they soften, about 5 more minutes.

Step 3: Into this mixture, add the celery and carrots, and then the mushrooms. Continue cooking until the mushrooms brown slightly and lose their water.

Step 4: Add the broth and bring to a boil. Reduce heat to simmer and add cabbage. Add water to the pot to cover the cabbage.

Step 5: Simmer soup for about an hour, covered. Remove from heat and let cool about 10 to 15 minutes before serving.

Nutritional Information

Calories 185		Total Carbohydrates 28.5mg	10%
Calories from Fat 39		Dietary Fiber 8.5 g	34%
	% Daily Value	Sugars 13.9mg	
Total Fat 4.3 g	7%	Protein 10.2 g	
Saturated Fat 0.8 g	4%	Vitamin A	270%
Trans Fat		Vitamin C	164%
Cholesterol 0mg	0%	Calcium	11%
Sodium 1354mg	56%	Iron	17%

Roasted Tomato and Basil Soup

Total Calories Per Serving: 133

Tomato and basil lovers rejoice! Here's a lovely new way to enjoy the summery flavors of that celebrated salad—with a spoon. Because this soup is so low-cal, you could even sneak a snack of a part-skim mozzarella string cheese stick (only about 70 calories) and get the full caprese salad effect.

Makes 4 Servings

Ingredients

2 tablespoons olive oil

2 teaspoons salt

1 teaspoon black pepper

1 package (about 8) campari tomatoes, quartered

2 medium onions, finely chopped

4 cloves garlic, minced

20 basil leaves, chopped, with stems removed

2 cups low-sodium vegetable stock

Directions

Step 1: Preheat oven to 400°.

Step 2: In a medium sized bowl, toss tomato quarters in 1 tablespoon of the olive oil. Place tomatoes, skin side down, in a glass casserole baking dish or similar. Roast about 40 minutes, until soft.

Step 3: While the tomatoes are roasting, heat the other 1 tablespoon of olive oil in a large stock pot or dutch oven. Add the onions and sauté until soft, about 8 minutes. Add the garlic and continue to sauté an additional 2 minutes.

Step 4: Add the tomatoes and basil to the pot and simmer for about 10 minutes. Add the vegetable stock and simmer, covered, for about 30 minutes.

Step 5: Remove from heat and allow to cool for at least 20 to 25 minutes. Blend until smooth with a hand mixer or pour cooled mixture into a blender and blend until smooth. Ladle into bowls and garnish with additional basil leaves, if desired.

Nutritional Information

Calories 133		Total Carbohydrates 15.2 g	5%
Calories from Fat 69		Dietary Fiber 4 g	16%
	% Daily Value	Sugars 8.5 g	
Total Fat 7.7 g	12%	Protein 3.2 g	
Saturated Fat 1.1 g	5%	Vitamin A	3%
Trans Fat		Vitamin C	92%
Cholesterol 0mg	0%	Calcium	2%
Sodium 394mg	16%	Iron	21%

Fast-tastic French Onion Soup

Total Calories Per Serving: 254

This mini-crock classic gets a nice, low-sodium, low-fat makeover with this version. If you want to be fancy, consider using low-fat gruyere cheese instead of swiss. They're similar in texture and flavor, though gruyere tends to be creamier—even the low-fat type.

Makes 8 servings

Ingredients

2 teaspoons olive oil
4 cups sweet onion, sliced into slivers
4 cups red onion, sliced into slivers
½ teaspoon freshly ground black pepper
¼ teaspoon salt

¼ cup dry white wine
8 cups beef broth
¼ teaspoon chopped fresh thyme
8 slices French bread, toasted and cut into 1-inch cubes
8 slices low-fat swiss cheese

Directions

Step 1: In a large stock pot or dutch oven, heat the olive oil on high until it's just smoking, then reduce heat to medium.

Step 2: Add the onions and sauté until soft, about 8 minutes. Next, stir in pepper and salt. Reduce heat to medium and cook, uncovered, for 20 minutes, stirring frequently.

Step 3: Turn up the heat and sauté an additional five minutes to caramelize onions, then deglaze the mixture by adding wine and cooking an additional 1 to 2 minutes.

Step 4: Add broth and bring to a boil. Reduce heat to simmer and stir in thyme. Cover and simmer 2 hours.

Step 5: Preheat broiler and spoon soup into 8 mini crocks. Crumble the cubed, toasted French bread into each. Place crocks on cookie sheet and top each with 1 slice of cheese. Broil, watching carefully, about 2-3 minutes. Remove from oven, cool slightly, and serve.

Nutritional Information

Calories 254		Total Carbohydrates 30.9mg	10%
Calories from Fat 64		Dietary Fiber 3.1 g	12%
	% Daily Value	Sugars 6.4 g	
Total Fat 7.1 g	11%	Protein 16.8 g	
Saturated Fat 2.7 g	14%	Vitamin A	6%
Trans Fat		Vitamin C	19%
Cholesterol 15mg	5%	Calcium	28%
Sodium 1075mg	45%	Iron	10%

THE 5:2 FAST DIET COOKBOOK

Spicy Zucchini Soup

Total Calories Per Serving: 136

Plain old zucchini gets sassed up with cilantro and spice in this savory soup. If you prefer a little less heat in your soup, you can always eliminate one of the jalapeño peppers and still enjoy a nice zip!

Makes 4 Servings

Ingredients

3 tablespoons butter

1 medium onion, chopped

2 cloves garlic, minced

5 medium zucchini, chopped

2 jalapeño peppers, minced

1 tablespoon salt

4 cups water

1 bunch cilantro

Directions

Step 1: In a large stock pot or dutch oven, heat the butter until it melts, then reduce heat to medium.

Step 2: Add the onions and sauté until soft, about 8 minutes, then the garlic and sauté an additional 2 minutes.

Step 3: Add the zucchini and jalapeños and sauté until zucchini softens, about 8 minutes.

Step 4: Add water and salt and bring to a boil. Reduce heat to medium and cook, uncovered, for 20 minutes, stirring frequently.

Step 5: Remove from heat and allow to cool for 20 to 25 minutes. Blend until smooth with a hand mixer, or pour cooled mixture into a blender and pulse until smooth. Divide among four bowls and serve warm, topped with cilantro.

Nutritional Information

Calories 136		Total Carbohydrates 12.7 g	4%
Calories from Fat 83		Dietary Fiber 3.9 g	15%
	% Daily Value	Sugars 6.1 g	
Total Fat 9.2 g	14%	Protein 3.8 g	
Saturated Fat 5.6 g	28%	Vitamin A	26%
Trans Fat		Vitamin C	79%
Cholesterol 23mg	8%	Calcium	5%
Sodium 2024mg	84%	Iron	7%

Potato Leek Lite Soup

Total Calories Per Serving: 294

Potato Leek soup is a deliciously satisfying dish, but a low-cal treat it is not. Here's a version that is just as enjoyable and filling that eliminates cream but still maintains a smooth, creamy texture.

Makes 6 Servings

Ingredients

4 teaspoons olive oil
1 medium onion, finely chopped
6 leeks, washed and chopped
6 cups chicken stock
8 medium potatoes, peeled and chopped
Salt and pepper, to taste

Directions

Step 1: In a large stock pot or dutch oven, heat the olive oil on high until it's just smoking, then reduce heat to medium.

Step 2: Add the onions and leeks and sauté until soft, about 8-10 minutes.

Step 3: Add chicken stock to the pot and bring to a boil. When the stock boils, add the potatoes and bring back to a boil. Then reduce heat to low, cover, and simmer 25-30 minutes, until potatoes get soft.

Step 4: Remove from heat and allow to cool for 20 to 25 minutes. Season with salt and pepper and blend until smooth with a hand mixer, or pour cooled mixture into a blender and pulse until smooth. Divide among bowls and serve warm.

Nutritional Information

Calories 294		Total Carbohydrates 59.7 g	20%
Calories from Fat 38		Dietary Fiber 8.8g	35%
	% Daily Value	Sugars 8.2g	
Total Fat 4.2 g	6%	Protein 7g	
Saturated Fat 0.7 g	3%	Vitamin A	31%
Trans Fat		Vitamin C	116%
Cholesterol 0mg	0%	Calcium	9%
Sodium 826mg	33%	Iron	19%

Cheesy Cauliflower Soup

Total Calories Per Serving: 259

Many have used cauliflower in dishes that typically call for white potatoes with excellent results. Here, what would have been a bucket-load of calories for a traditional potato au gratin soup is now a satisfyingly manageable 259 calories. (This recipe also features another one of my favorite substitutes—turkey bacon for extra flavor!)

Makes 2 Servings

Ingredients

1½ tablespoons extra virgin olive oil
¼ cup onions, chopped
2 cloves garlic, minced
1½ cup reduced sodium chicken broth
1 head cauliflower, chopped into florets
½ cup unsweetened almond milk
⅓ cup cheddar cheese
3 slices turkey bacon, cooked crisp and crumbled

Directions

Step 1: In a large stock pot or dutch oven, heat the olive oil on high until it's just smoking, then reduce heat to medium.

Step 2: Add the onions and sauté until soft, about 8 minutes. Add garlic and sauté an additional 2 minutes.

Step 3: Add chicken broth and bring to a boil. Next, add cauliflower florets. When the pot comes to a boil again, lower heat to low, cover and simmer for 30 minutes or until cauliflower is tender.

Step 4: Remove from heat and allow to cool for 20 minutes. Blend until smooth with a hand mixer, or pour cooled mixture into a blender and pulse until smooth, gradually adding almond milk. Divide among four bowls, garnish with cheese and turkey bacon, and serve warm.

Nutritional Information

Calories 259		Total Carbohydrates 10.9mg	4%
Calories from Fat 167		Dietary Fiber 3.9mg	16%
	% Daily Value	Sugars 4.8g	
Total Fat 18.6g	28%	Protein 13.2g	
Saturated Fat 5.5g	27%	Vitamin A	7%
Trans Fat		Vitamin C	112%
Cholesterol 35mg	12%	Calcium	28%
Sodium 811mg	33%	Iron	5%

Roasted Asparagus and Onion Soup

Total Calories Per Serving: 142

Asparagus lovers are in for a treat with this simple soup. Less than 20 calories in 5 spears of asparagus, which is about the serving size here.

Makes 4 Servings

Ingredients

2 tablespoons olive oil

1 bunch of asparagus (about 20 spears)

1 tablespoon Herbs de Provence

Pinch of salt

Dash of pepper

1 medium red onion, chopped

2 cloves garlic, minced

1 tablespoon tarragon

3½ cups low-sodium chicken broth

½ cup soy milk

Directions

Step 1: Preheat oven to 425°. In a glass casserole baking dish, toss asparagus with some olive oil, salt, pepper, and Herbs de Provence. Roast at 425° for 12-15 minutes, until asparagus is just soft. Remove from oven and cool. Slice into bite-sized bits.

Step 2: While the asparagus is roasting, in a large stock pot or dutch oven, heat the 2 tablespoons of olive oil on high until it's just smoking, then reduce heat to medium. Add the onions and sauté until soft, about 8 minutes. Add garlic and tarragon and sauté an additional 2 minutes.

Step 3: Add chicken broth and chopped asparagus and bring to a boil. Reduce heat to low and cover. Simmer 15-20 minutes, so the flavors meld.

Step 4: Remove from heat and let cool 20-25 minutes. Blend with a hand mixer until smooth, or pour into a blender and pulse. In either instance, add the soy milk gradually while you blend.

Step 5: Return to pan to reheat. Serve warm.

Nutritional Information

Calories 118	Total Carbohydrates 8.6 g	
Calories from Fat 69	Dietary Fiber 2.2 g	
% Daily Value	Sugars 3.6 g	
Total Fat 7.7 g	Protein 4.7 g	
Saturated Fat 1.1 g	Vitamin A	11%
Trans Fat	Vitamin C	12%
Cholesterol 0mg	Calcium	3%
Sodium 118mg	Iron	12%

Updated Classic Chicken Soup

Total Calories Per Serving: 210

A new spin on an old favorite which, even not doctored, is still a light and nutritious way to enjoy chicken and veggies. Here, chicken sausage is added to the mix to lend a salty, smoky flavor.

Makes 4 Servings

Ingredients

3 tablespoons olive oil

Salt and pepper

8 ounces skinless, boneless chicken breast, cut into small cubes

1 chicken sausage, pre-cooked, sliced into discs, then quartered

1 leek, finely chopped

8 ounces mushrooms, roughly chopped

1 cup fennel, sliced

2 cups reduced-fat, low-sodium chicken broth

Directions

Step 1: In a large stock pot or dutch oven, heat two tablespoons of olive oil on high until it's just smoking, then reduce heat to medium. Season the chicken breast with salt and pepper and drop into the hot pot. Sauté about 5 minutes, until the chicken is cooked through. Add the chicken sausage and cook another 1-2 minutes. Remove with a slotted spoon and set aside.

Step 2: In the same pot, add the rest of the olive oil and then the leeks. Sauté until the leeks are soft, about 6 minutes.

Step 3: Next add the fennel and mushrooms and sauté until the mushrooms brown and lose their water, and the fennel wilts, about 6-7 minutes.

Step 4: Add the chicken broth and bring to a boil. Reduce heat and simmer 30-35 minutes. Remove from heat and serve.

Nutritional Information

Calories 210		Total Carbohydrates 9.2 g	3%
Calories from Fat 71		Dietary Fiber 2.2 g	8%
	% Daily Value	Sugars 3.2 g	
Total Fat 7.9 g	16%	Protein 26.5	
Saturated Fat 1.0 g	9%	Vitamin A	13%
Trans Fat		Vitamin C	28%
Cholesterol 64mg	17%	Calcium	5%
Sodium 960mg	11%	Iron	21%

Classic Veggie Soup

Total Calories Per Serving: 151

Good for you and easy to prepare, Classic Vegetable Soup is a staple of home cooking. This version is not only delicious but packed with healthy doses of vitamins A and C.

Makes 6-10 servings

Ingredients

2 teaspoons olive oil

1 cup sweet onion, chopped

1¾ cups leeks, chopped

2 carrots, sliced

1 large tomato, peeled, seeded, and chopped

1 large potato, peeled and diced into cubes

Salt and pepper

Dash of ground thyme

½ cup canned navy beans

6 cups water

2 large zucchini, diced

¾ cup uncooked pasta

¼ pound green beans, trimmed and cut crosswise in half

Directions

Step 1: Coat a large skillet in the olive oil and heat over medium-high heat. Add onions, then leeks, then sauté 3-4 minutes. Next add the carrots, tomatoes, and potato, and sauté an additional 5-7 minutes. Season with ground thyme, and salt and pepper, making sure to cover all the vegetables.

Step 2: Transfer all ingredients to a large pot and add the water. Bring to a boil, then reduce heat and simmer for about 45 minutes, until the potatoes and carrots are tender.

Step 3: Stir in navy beans, zucchini, pasta, and green beans and cook until pasta is tender (check cooking instructions on package for a guide). Serve warm.

Nutritional Information

Calories 151		Total Carbohydrates 30.6mg	10%
Calories from Fat 6		Dietary Fiber 7.5 g	30%
	% Daily Value	Sugars 5.1 g	
Total Fat 0.7 g	1%	Protein 7.1 g	
Saturated Fat		Vitamin A	76%
Trans Fat		Vitamin C	39%
Cholesterol 0mg	0%	Calcium	8%
Sodium 626mg	26%	Iron	16%

Orzo Minestrone

Total Calories Per Serving: 230

Here's a slightly exotic turn on the Classic Vegetable Soup. It's also jam-packed with healthy ingredients and light on calories. An added bonus: using a slow cooker makes it a snap to prepare!

Makes 4 Servings

Ingredients

4 cups fat-free vegetable broth
⅔ cup zucchini, cut into ½-inch discs
½ cup green onions, sliced
2 teaspoons marjoram
Salt and pepper
2 cups cabbage, shredded
1½ cups carrots, chopped
2 cloves garlic, finely chopped
18 ounces of canned crushed tomatoes
1 large yellow sweet pepper, cut into ½-inch chunks
⅔ cup orzo
4 tablespoons fresh basil, chopped

Directions

Step 1: Add all ingredients, less the orzo and basil, to a 6-quart slow cooker. Cover and set heat to low. Cook for 6 to 8 hours.

Step 2: In the last 20 minutes, set a pot of water to boil on the stove and prepare orzo according to package directions.

Step 3: Drain orzo and add to cooker, along with basil. Cover and continue to cook on low for another 15 to 20 minutes..

Nutritional Information

Calories 230			Total Carbohydrates 47.7 g	16%
Calories from Fat 9			Dietary Fiber 8.7 g	35%
		% Daily Value	Sugars 15.7	
Total Fat 1 g		1%	Protein 8.5 g	
Saturated Fat			Vitamin A	221%
Trans Fat			Vitamin C	205%
Cholesterol 0mg		0%	Calcium	11%
Sodium 1193mg		50%	Iron	22%

Border-ing on Awesome Toruntila Soup

Total Calories Per Serving: 159

In the mood for Mexican tonight? It's hard to believe that something so good can be so good for you too, but when made with chicken sausage, this yummy toruntila soup clocks in at only 159 calories! This recipe takes a little work but the results are well worth it.

Makes 4-6 Servings

Ingredients

3 soft corn toruntilas

1 tablespoon olive oil

1 small white onion, chopped

6 ounces chicken sausage

1½ teaspoons dried oregano

1 tablespoon ground dried chili

1 teaspoon ground cumin

14 ounces no-salt-added, diced canned tomatoes

3 cups low-sodium chicken broth

Directions

Step 1: Preheat oven to 375°F.

Step 2: Lay out toruntilas and lightly brush with olive oil. Cut toruntilas into 1 to 2-inch strips. Arrange on a baking sheet and bake until crisp, about 12 to 15 minutes.

Step 3: While the toruntilas are crisping, add the remaining olive oil to a large stock pot or dutch oven and heat on medium to high heat. Add onion and sauté until softened, about 5-7 minutes.

Step 4: While onion is sautéing, remove sausages from their casings. Crumble the sausage into the pan with the onion and continue cooking until the sausage browns, about 5 minutes.

Step 5: Now stir in spice and add tomatoes. Let the tomatoes cook with the spices and sausage-onion mixture about a minute or two, then add the broth. Bring to a boil, reduce heat, cover and simmer for an additional 20 to 25 minutes.

Step 6: Remove soup from heat and serve with crispy toruntila strips.

Nutritional Information

Calories 159		Total Carbohydrates 25.6 g	9%
Calories from Fat 23		Dietary Fiber 6.2 g	25%
	% Daily Value	Sugars 1.2 g	
Total Fat 2.6 g	4%	Protein 12.7 g	
Saturated Fat 0.6 g	3%	Vitamin A	34%
Trans Fat		Vitamin C	50%
Cholesterol 24mg	8%	Calcium	12%
Sodium 555mg	23%	Iron	23%

Chill-Out Corn Soup with Shrimp

Total Calories Per Serving: 278

A great warm weather recipe or for times you just don't feel like having hot soup. Shrimp and leeks make this dish an extravagant treat without piling on the calories, and using coconut oil versus a more traditional oil gives the soup a nice kick!

Makes 3-4 Servings

Ingredients

1 tablespoon coconut oil
2 large leeks, white and light green parts, thinly sliced
3 cups corn
2 cups low-sodium vegetable broth
1 cup water
1 avocado, diced
6 ounces of grape tomatoes, quartered lengthwise
8 to 10 leaves basil, shredded
Cooking spray
8 ounces of small or medium shrimp
Salt and pepper
The juice of 1 lime

Directions

Step 1: In a large stock pot or dutch oven, heat oil over medium to high heat. Add leeks and sauté for 7 to 9 minutes, until softened. Add corn to the pot and toss well with leeks, and cook together for an additional 2 to 3 minutes.

Step 2: Add the broth to the pot and bring to a boil. Now reduce heat to low, cover, and simmer about 25 to 30 minutes.

Step 3: Remove pot from heat and allow soup to cool for 10 to 15 minutes. When soup has cooled, either purée with a hand mixer or in batches in a food processor or blender. Pour soup into a large covered bowl and chill for at least 4 hours.

Step 4: Just before you're ready to remove puréed soup from the refrigerator, toss avocado, tomato, and basil together in a small bowl.

Continued . . .

Step 5: Next, heat a nonstick skillet on medium and coat with cooking spray. Toss shrimp into skillet, seasoning with salt and pepper and cooking until opaque, about 2 to 3 minutes per side. Set aside to cool.

Step 6: Stir lime juice into purée, add the avocado, tomato, and shredded basil mixture, plus the cooled shrimp, and serve.

Nutritional Information

Calories 278		Total Carbohydrates 24.9mg	8%
Calories from Fat 117		Dietary Fiber 6 g	24%
	% Daily Value	Sugars 5.4 g	
Total Fat 13 g	20%	Protein 18.9 g	
Saturated Fat 4.6 g	23%	Vitamin A	21%
Trans Fat		Vitamin C	41%
Cholesterol 119mg	40%	Calcium	9%
Sodium 652mg	27%	Iron	21%

Totally Hot and Sour Shrimp Soup

Total Calories Per Serving: 247

An exotic soup that brings together several favorite flavors of the Far East, here's a guilt-free alternative to the usual Chinese take-out— and the simple preparation will get this soup to your table faster than any delivery person!

Makes 4 Servings

Ingredients

3 cups fat-free, reduced-sodium chicken broth

½ cup mushrooms, sliced

1 tablespoon low-sodium soy sauce

1 (8-ounce) can sliced bamboo shoots, drained

2½ tablespoons fresh lemon juice

1 teaspoon white pepper

1½ pounds medium shrimp

8 ounces reduced-fat firm tofu, drained and cut into 1-inch cubes

1 tablespoon cornstarch

2 tablespoons water

1 large egg white, beaten

¼ teaspoon chili oil

2 tablespoons chopped green onions

Directions

Step 1: Heat a large stockpot or dutch oven on medium-high heat and add the broth, mushrooms, soy sauce, and bamboo shoots. Bring to a boil, then reduce heat to low. Simmer for 5 minutes.

Step 2: Now add lemon juice, pepper, shrimp, and tofu to pan and bring to a boil. Boil the soup about 2-4 minutes, or until shrimp are opaque.

Step 3: While the soup is boiling, mix cornstarch with water in a small bowl, making a loose paste. Spoon the paste into the soup and cook a minute or 2, stirring constantly with a whisk, until the soup thickens.

Step 4: Once the soup thickens, slowly drizzle in egg white, stirring all the while. Remove from heat; stir in chili oil and onions, and serve.

Nutritional Information

Calories 247		Total Carbohydrates 8.3 g	3%
Calories from Fat 49		Dietary Fiber 1.7 g	9%
	% Daily Value	Sugars 2.5 g	
Total Fat 5.5 g	8%	Protein 40.1 g	
Saturated Fat 1.4 g	3%	Vitamin A	9%
Trans Fat		Vitamin C	10%
Cholesterol 287mg	111%	Calcium	23%
Sodium 991mg	40%	Iron	12%

Spicy Thai Chicken Soup

Total Calories Per Serving: 205

Spice up your life with Asian-inspired soup that gets its heat from a healthy dose of red-pepper flakes. If you're feeling especially spicy, you can also stir in some Sriracha sauce, a blazing-hot blend of chili peppers and spices from Southeast Asia. Proceed with caution—just a little Sriracha will spice things up quickly!

Makes 4 Servings

Ingredients

1 ounce cellophane noodles
8 ounces chicken breasts, skinless and boneless
1 tablespoon peanut oil
2 teaspoons minced garlic
2 teaspoons minced ginger
¼ teaspoon red pepper flakes
28 ounces chicken broth
2 tablespoons low-sodium soy sauce
2 tablespoons chopped fresh cilantro
2 tablespoons chopped green onions
1 tablespoon chopped fresh basil
Sriracha sauce (optional)

Directions

Step 1: Soak noodles in very hot tap water. While the noodles are soaking, trim all excess fat off the chicken and slice into thin strips.

Step 2: In dutch oven or large stock pot, heat the peanut oil over medium-high heat. When the oil is hot, add the chicken strips, garlic, ginger, and pepper flakes to the skillet.

Step 3: Sauté ingredients together in the pan for 2-3 minutes, until the chicken starts to brown. Now add broth and soy sauce and bring to a boil.

Step 4: Reduce heat to medium and simmer another 8 to 10 minutes, until the chicken is fully cooked. Remove from heat.

Step 5: Now drain the cellophane noodles and add to the pot. Serve with cilantro, onion, and basil, and stir in Sriracha sauce, or a hot sauce of your choosing, if desired.

Nutritional Information

Calories 205		Total Carbohydrates 8.8 g	3%
Calories from Fat 79		Dietary Fiber	
	% Daily Value	Sugars 1.2 g	
Total Fat 8.8 g	14%	Protein 21.2 g	
Saturated Fat 2.1 g	10%	Vitamin A	4%
Trans Fat		Vitamin C	3%
Cholesterol 50 mg	17%	Calcium	3%
Sodium 1377 mg	47%	Iron	9%

Thai Lemongrass Soup

Total Calories Per Serving: 260

A staple of traditional Thai cuisine, lemongrass soup is a simple but delicious dish which can accompany a larger meal, or, in this case, stand beautifully and satisfyingly on its own.

Makes 2 Servings

Ingredients

- 1 cup rice noodles
- 2 cups water
- 2 tablespoons lemongrass chili paste
- 1 chicken breast, sliced into slivers
- ½ cup kale, chopped
- 4 mushrooms, sliced
- 1 tablespoon lime juice

Directions

Step 1: Prepare rice noodles per instructions on package. Drain and set aside.

Step 2: In a large stock pot or dutch oven, bring the 2 cups of water to a boil. Add the lemongrass chili paste and immediately reduce heat to low.

Step 3: While the lemongrass broth is simmering, add in the chicken breast and kale. Cook about 7 to 9 minutes, until the chicken is cooked all the way through.

Step 4: Now add the noodles, mushrooms, and lime juice and simmer about 7 to 10 additional minutes. Serve and enjoy.

Nutritional Information

Calories 260		Total Carbohydrates 26.4 g	9%
Calories from Fat 31		Dietary Fiber 1.6 g	7%
	% Daily Value	Sugars 0.8 g	
Total Fat 3.5 g	5%	Protein 30.2 g	
Saturated Fat		Vitamin A	53%
Trans Fat		Vitamin C	44%
Cholesterol 74mg	25%	Calcium	5%
Sodium 655mg	27%	Iron	16%

Easy Crab Soup

Total Calories Per Serving: 213

Healthy eating doesn't get any easier than this no fuss, no muss simple crab soup. If you can boil water, you can make this soup. Tasty, low-calorie, and oh-so-easy, it's as win-win as home cooking gets.

Makes 2 Servings

Ingredients

1 teaspoon Old Bay seasoning
2 vegetable bouillon cubes
1 clove garlic
½ cup purple onion, diced
1 10-ounce package of frozen mixed vegetables
10 ounces of tomatoes, peeled, seeded, and diced
4 cups water
6 ounces of real crab meat
Salt and pepper, to taste

Directions

Step 1: Add all ingredients into a large stockpot or Dutch oven. Bring to a boil and simmer for 30 minutes.

Step 2: Season with salt and pepper and serve.

Nutritional Information

		% Daily Value			
Calories 213			Total Carbohydrates 29		10%
Calories from Fat 21			Dietary Fiber 8.4 g		34%
			Sugars 9.8 g		
Total Fat 2.3 g		4%	Protein 16.8 g		
Saturated Fat			Vitamin A		118%
Trans Fat			Vitamin C		63%
Cholesterol 46mg		15%	Calcium		36%
Sodium 1532mg		64%	Iron		26%

Greek Lemon Rice Soup

Total Calories Per Serving: 292

In less than 20 minutes, and for fewer than 300 calories, you can enjoy a taste of the Greek Isles in this savory soup that combines traditional ingredients of Greek fare. All the flavor of your favorite *taverna* without any of the guilt. *Opa!*

Makes 2-3 servings

Ingredients

4 cups reduced-sodium chicken broth
⅓ cup white rice
1½ slices silken tofu
1 tablespoon olive oil
¼ teaspoon turmeric
¼ cup lemon juice
2 tablespoon dill
¼ teaspoon freshly ground pepper

Directions

Step 1: Heat a large stock pot or dutch oven over medium-high heat and add broth and rice to the pot. Bring to a boil, then reduce heat to low. Simmer until the rice is very tender, about 15 minutes. Remove from heat and let cool.

Step 2: Transfer soft rice with a slotted spoon to a blender or food processor, keeping remaining liquid in the pot.

Step 3: Add tofu, oil, and turmeric to the rice and process until smooth. Transfer to a bowl and whisk this mixture with the lemon juice, dill, and pepper into the remaining liquid in the pot. Reheat and serve warm.

Nutritional Information

Calories 292		Total Carbohydrates 30.2	10%
Calories from Fat 103		Dietary Fiber 1.1 g	4%
	% Daily Value	Sugars 2.6 g	
Total Fat 11.5 g	18%	Protein 15.7 g	
Saturated Fat 2.3 g	11%	Vitamin A	4%
Trans Fat		Vitamin C	26%
Cholesterol 0mg	0%	Calcium	10%
Sodium 1556mg	65%	Iron	25%

Not So Shabby Crabby Bisque

Total Calories Per Serving: 250

Often thought of as caloric disaster, creamy bisques can be very satisfying when prepared with an eye to calorie caution. This low-calorie alternative has all the flavor of the creamy concoctions you love. Consider spicing things up by garnishing with Old Bay seasoning instead of the paprika.

Makes 6 Servings

Ingredients

1 avocado, diced
2 cups corn
1 tomato, seeded and diced
1 tablespoon lime juice
¾ teaspoon salt
1 tablespoon extra-virgin olive oil
1 cup onion, chopped
1 cup yellow bell pepper, diced

1½ cups russet potato, peeled and diced
1 teaspoon paprika
1 cup dry vermouth
2 cups seafood stock
2 cups low-fat milk
12 ounces crabmeat, drained
Freshly ground pepper, to taste

Directions

Step 1: Combine avocado, 1 cup of the corn, tomato, lime juice, pepper, and ¼ teaspoon of salt in a small bowl. Toss to coat all ingredients in the lime juice. Set aside this relish.

Step 2: In a large stockpot or dutch oven heat olive oil over medium heat. Add onion and bell pepper and sauté until softened, about 5 minutes.

Step 3: Add the remaining cup of corn and sauté an additional 2 to 3 minutes. Then add potato and paprika and cook, stirring often, for 2 minutes.

Step 4: Now add vermouth and scrape up browned bits, and stir until the liquid reduces slightly, about 5 minutes.

Step 5: Add stock and bring to a boil. Reduce heat to low and simmer, stirring occasionally, until the potatoes are very tender, about 20 to 25 minutes. Remove from heat and cool.

Step 6: In batches, add the mixture to a blender or food processor, and purée until smooth.

Step 7: Return the purée to the pot and stir in milk, crab, and remaining salt. Cook, stirring occasionally, until the crab is heated all the way through, 3 to 5 minutes. Add the relish and sprinkle with paprika (or Old Bay seasoning, if you choose) and serve.

Nutritional Information

Calories 250		Total Carbohydrates 31.2 g	10%
Calories from Fat 83		Dietary Fiber 4.9 g	19%
	% Daily Value	Sugars 11.6 g	
Total Fat 9.2mg	14%	Protein 11.4 g	
Saturated Fat 1.8 g	9%	Vitamin A	14%
Trans Fat		Vitamin C	55%
Cholesterol 15mg	5%	Calcium	11%
Sodium 772mg	32%	Iron	13%

Chapter 4: Meats and Other Proteins

When you haven't had very much to eat all day, dinner definitely takes on a whole new urgency! After being good and fasting since breakfast, you really want to have something more to look forward to than a handful of carrot sticks and celery stalks and a tall glass of water. Hopefully this chapter will give you the inspiration you need to get through the day!

The great thing about doing the 5:2 Fast Diet is that as long as you stay within your calorie range (remember, 600 calories for men and 500 calories for women), you're free to eat what you want. Remember, to feel satisfied and full it's important to take in calories that are full of nutrients.

You don't need to eschew steak or pork on the 5:2 Fast Diet. You don't need to say goodbye to savory sauces and creams. What you do need to do is to eat within portion parameters that are measured and reasonable, and to use ingredients in cooking that save you calories where it doesn't matter so you can really enjoy indulging in extra calories where it does.

Spicy-Sweet Chicken

Total Calories Per Serving: 251

A glaze of ginger and a kick of cayenne make this chicken a pleaser for lots of palates. Serve with a side salad or enjoy with the Zucchini Pasta on page 199.

Makes 4 Servings

Ingredients

4 chicken breasts, skinless, boneless and trimmed of excess fat

Cooking spray

Salt and pepper

2 tablespoons honey

2 tablespoons dijon mustard

4 tablespoons water

2-3 teaspoons ground ginger

2-4 garlic cloves, peeled and crushed

Pinch of cayenne pepper

Directions

Step 1: Preheat oven to 350°. Lightly coat the bottom of a glass oven-proof casserole dish with cooking spray and set aside. Season chicken breasts with salt and pepper.

Step 2: In a medium bowl, mix together the honey, dijon mustard, water, ginger, garlic, and cayenne pepper. Dunk each piece of chicken individually into this mixture and toss to coat. Place each piece of chicken in the baking dish.

Step 3: Place chicken in oven and bake 30 minutes, making sure they are cooked through before removing from oven. Serve with juices, if desired.

Nutritional Information

Calories 251		Total Carbohydrates 10.8 g	4%
Calories from Fat 79		Dietary Fiber 0.6 g	2%
	% Daily Value	Sugars 8.9 g	
Total Fat 8.8 g	14%	Protein 31.3 g	
Saturated Fat 2.2 g	11%	Vitamin A	2%
Trans Fat		Vitamin C	1%
Cholesterol 93mg	31%	Calcium	4%
Sodium 92mg	4%	Iron	10%

Tequila Lime Chicken

Total Calories Per Serving: 295

Yes, you can have tequila on a fast day . . . but only as part of a marinade, as it's used in this tangy and tasty dish.

Makes 6 Servings

Ingredients
½ cup tequila
1 cup lime juice
½ cup orange juice
3 cloves garlic, minced
Salt and pepper
6 chicken breasts, skinless and boneless
Cooking spray

Directions
Step 1: In a large bowl, whisk together the tequila, lime juice, orange juice, garlic, salt, and pepper.

Step 2: Trim the boneless chicken breasts of all fat and slice each, width-wise, into 2 or 3 pieces. Add the chicken to the marinade. Cover and refrigerate as little as 1 hour or overnight to maximize the marinade.

Step 3: Heat a grill pan over high heat and coat with cooking spray. Cook the chicken 7-8 minutes per side, until cooked through. Serve.

Nutritional Information

Calories 295		Total Carbohydrates 7 g	2%
Calories from Fat 81		Dietary Fiber 0.8 g	3%
	% Daily Value	Sugars 2.6 g	
Total Fat 9 g	14%	Protein 34.4 g	
Saturated Fat 2.4 g	12%	Vitamin A	10%
Trans Fat		Vitamin C	41%
Cholesterol 104mg	35%	Calcium	3%
Sodium 890mg	37%	Iron	10%

Chicken Cacciatore

Total Calories Per Serving: 291

A Sunday-style dinner any night of the week? This cacciatore recipe is certainly that simple. It's also a great way to enjoy good eating and stick to your fast if Sunday happens to be your fasting day. Using chicken breast and eliminating both skin and bones are a great way to reduce the calories in this savory favorite.

Makes 6-8 Servings

Ingredients

1 tablespoons olive oil

8 chicken thighs, skinless and boneless

Salt and pepper

2 tablespoons all-purpose flour

1 onion, diced

2 cloves garlic, minced

1 sweet red pepper, chopped

1 cup mushrooms, sliced

1 28 ounce can crushed tomatoes

½ cup sodium-reduced chicken stock

Directions

Step 1: Heat olive oil in a large dutch oven or stock pot over medium heat.

Step 2: Add flour to a plate and season with salt and pepper. Dredge the chicken, piece by piece, and, when oil is hot, add to the pot.

Step 3: Brown the chicken about 2-3 minutes per side. Remove from pot and set aside.

Step 4: Toss the onion into the pot and sauté in the pan drippings about 5-6 minutes, or until the onion is soft. Add the garlic and sauté an additional 2-3 minutes. Add pepper and sliced mushrooms and sautée until soft, about 4 minutes.

Step 5: Now add the canned tomatoes and stock and bring to a boil.

Step 6: Reduce heat and put chicken and any juices back into the pot. Simmer 45 minutes to an hour and serve warm.

Nutritional Information

Calories 291			Total Carbohydrates 12.3 g	4%
Calories from Fat 101			Dietary Fiber 4.0 g	16%
		% Daily Value	Sugars 7.0 g	
Total Fat 11.3 g		17%	Protein 33.8 g	
Saturated Fat 2.8 g		14%	Vitamin A	30%
Trans Fat			Vitamin C	47%
Cholesterol 93mg		31%	Calcium	7%
Sodium 462mg		19%	Iron	18%

Slow-Cooking Provence Chicken

Total Calories Per Serving: 266

French Women Don't Get Fat. It's not just the name of a popular book, it's a lifestyle! When you start to look at your food in the simplest sense, and make smart choices about how you prepare it—whole, natural foods made with simple, wholesome ingredients—you'll find your body shape reflecting your good choices, like with this basic Provence chicken dish.

Makes 4 servings

Ingredients
4 chicken breasts, skinless and boneless
2 teaspoons dried basil
Salt and pepper
1 cup yellow bell pepper, roughly chopped
8 ounces canned cannellini beans
14 ounces canned crushed tomatoes

Directions
Step 1: Trim chicken of excess fat and slice each breast into 2-3 pieces.

Step 2: Season the chicken with the basil, salt, and black pepper, and add to your slow cooker. Add the bell pepper, beans, and tomatoes. Cover and cook on low-heat setting for 8 hours.

Nutritional Information

Calories 266		Total Carbohydrates 26.2 g	9%
Calories from Fat 28		Dietary Fiber 10.6 g	42%
	% Daily Value	Sugars 3.2 g	
Total Fat 3.1 g	5%	Protein 33.8 g	
Saturated Fat		Vitamin A	10%
Trans Fat		Vitamin C	59%
Cholesterol 64mg	21%	Calcium	7%
Sodium 361mg	15%	Iron	29%

Orange Chipotle Chicken

Total Calories Per Serving: 227

Chipotle is hot, and not just on the tongue. Here, chipotle mingles with the sweet tang of oranges and the maple syrup, making a dish that's satisfying on so many levels.

Makes 4-6 Servings

Ingredients

1 teaspoon olive oil
4 chicken breasts, skinless and boneless
1 teaspoon chili powder
½ teaspoon ground cumin
1 tablespoon chipotle powder
Pinch of salt
⅓ cup light orange juice
2 tablespoons pure maple syrup
1 teaspoon orange zest

Directions

Step 1: Over medium heat, heat oil in a large nonstick skillet. Then toss together chili powder, cumin, chipotle powder, and salt and pour mixture on a plate.

Step 2: Trim chicken of all excess fat. Dredge chicken in spice mixture until nicely coated on all sides.

Step 3: Turn skillet up to medium high heat and add chicken. Cook 7-8 minutes per side, until chicken is cooked all the way through. Remove from pan and keep warm in a covered bowl.

Step 4: Add orange juice, orange zest, and maple syrup to the hot skillet. Heat on high to boil then turn back down to medium / medium-low. Cook until the liquid thickens, about 2 to 3 minutes.

Step 5: Add chicken and any juices back to pan. Toss chicken in sauce and warm for about a minute. Remove from heat and serve.

Nutritional Information

Calories 260		Total Carbohydrates 3.8 g	1%
Calories from Fat 60		Dietary Fiber 0.8 g	3%
	% Daily Value	Sugars 2.2 g	
Total Fat 6.7 g	10%	Protein 34.8 g	
Saturated Fat 1.5 g	8%	Vitamin A	68%
Trans Fat		Vitamin C	57%
Cholesterol 243mg	81%	Calcium	13%
Sodium 605mg	25%	Iron	16%

Grilled Lemon Chicken with Oregano

Total Calories Per Serving: 265

Lemon and chicken are a natural pair. Start with these as a base for a meal and not only are you headed in a health-conscious direction, you also have the base for a delicious treat. Here, the zip of oregano completes the experience.

Makes 4 Servings

Ingredients

The juice of 1 lemon

The zest of 1 lemon

1 bunch fresh oregano, chopped

Salt and pepper

1 tablespoon olive oil

4 chicken breasts, skinless and boneless

Cooking spray

Directions

Step 1: Combine lemon juice, lemon zest, oregano, olive oil, salt, and pepper in a large bowl. Whisk the ingredients together until well-combined and set aside.

Step 2: Trim chicken of all fat and slice each breast width-wise into 2 to 3 pieces. Place the chicken in the marinade and cover. Soak for half an hour at room temperature, or, for more flavorful chicken, overnight in the refrigerator.

Step 3: Heat a grill pan to high heat and coat in cooking spray. When grill pan is hot, place chicken in pan and cook thoroughly, about 7 minutes per side.

Nutritional Information

Calories 265		Total Carbohydrates 5.9 g	2%
Calories from Fat 101		Dietary Fiber 1.8 g	7%
	% Daily Value	Sugars 1.7 g	
Total Fat 11.3 g	17%	Protein 36.9 g	
Saturated Fat 1.1 g	5%	Vitamin A	0%
Trans Fat		Vitamin C	60%
Cholesterol 96mg	32%	Calcium	3%
Sodium 449mg	19%	Iron	10%

Baked Chicken and Peppers

Total Calories Per Serving: 241

Chicken thigh meat is higher in calories than breast meat, so you want to take extra care in both the portion you eat and the ingredients you add to it. Here, simple peppers have very little effect on the calories you'll take in.

Makes 4-6 Servings

Ingredients

4 chicken thighs, skinless
4 chicken legs, skinless
3 yellow bell peppers
2 red bell peppers

1 tablespoons olive oil
1 clove garlic, minced
Salt and pepper

Directions

Step 1: Preheat oven to 350°. Core and rinse peppers of all seeds and slice into strips. Set aside.

Step 2: Add chicken thighs and legs to a glass casserole dish. Toss chicken with pepper strips, olive oil, garlic, and salt and pepper, until the chicken and peppers are well coated.

Step 3: Roast chicken and peppers for 50 minutes, or until cooked through. Remove from oven and serve.

Nutritional Information

Calories 241		Total Carbohydrates 6.2 g	2%
Calories from Fat 137		Dietary Fiber 1.7 g	7%
	% Daily Value	Sugars 3.3 g	
Total Fat 15.2 g	23%	Protein 19.4 g	
Saturated Fat 1.5 g	8%	Vitamin A	48%
Trans Fat		Vitamin C	159%
Cholesterol 48mg	16%	Calcium	1%
Sodium 193mg	8%	Iron	5%

Spicy Chicken with Mango

Total Calories Per Serving: 229

What's better than a fun, quick, and highly exotic dish made with less than five ingredients?

Makes 4 Servings

Ingredients
⅓ cup coconut milk
1 teaspoon red curry paste
1 tablespoon fish sauce
Cooking spray
1 cup mango chunks
1 pound chicken thighs, skinless and boneless

Directions
Step 1: In a medium sized bowl, whisk together the coconut milk, red curry paste, and fish sauce. Set the sauce aside.

Step 2: Trim fat from chicken thighs and slice into cubes. Set the chicken aside.

Step 3: Coat a large nonstick skillet with cooking spray and set over medium-high heat. Add the chicken cubes and sauté approximately 5 minutes, just until the chicken is browned.

Step 4: Add the sauce to the chicken and turn down heat to low. Simmer, covered, for 5 to 10 minutes. Remove from heat, stir in mango chunks, and serve.

Nutritional Information

Calories 229		Total Carbohydrates 10.7 g	4%
Calories from Fat 102		Dietary Fiber 1.4 g	6%
	% Daily Value	Sugars 8.5 g	
Total Fat 11.3 g	17%	Protein 21.1 g	
Saturated Fat 6.1 g	30%	Vitamin A	9%
Trans Fat		Vitamin C	25%
Cholesterol 62 mg	21%	Calcium	2%
Sodium 491 mg	20%	Iron	8%

Light Chicken Stew

Total Calories Per Serving: 235

We sometimes think of stews as being heavy, winter-time foods that we should avoid when trying to lose weight, but a stew like this one—which is more like a soup with less liquid—is exactly the kind of meal that will fill your belly without filling out your jeans.

Makes 4 to 6 Servings

Ingredients

6 chicken thighs

2 cups carrot, sliced

1 leek

1 tablespoon chopped fresh tarragon

1 cup reduced-fat, reduced sodium chicken stock

4 ounces dry vermouth

1 tablespoon flour

½ teaspoon salt

8 ounces fresh asparagus, cut in 1-inch pieces

½ cup peas

Directions

Step 1: Place chicken, carrots, leek, and tarragon in slow-cooker.

Step 2: Add low-fat chicken stock, vermouth, and flour. Toss to coat. Cover and cook on low 5 to 8 hours, until tender.

Step 3: Turn cooker to high heat. Add asparagus. Now cover and cook on high about 10 minutes, or until the asparagus are slightly tender.

Step 4: Turn off cooker and pour stew into a bowl. Stir in peas to warm and serve.

Nutritional Information

Calories 235		Total Carbohydrates 8.8 g	3%
Calories from Fat 64		Dietary Fiber 2.2 g	9%
	% Daily Value	Sugars 3 g	
Total Fat 7.1 g	11%	Protein 28.6 g	
Saturated Fat 1.9 g	10%	Vitamin A	134%
Trans Fat		Vitamin C	10%
Cholesterol 83mg	28%	Calcium	5%
Sodium 423 g	28%	Iron	14%

Chicken a la King—That's King!

Total Calories Per Serving: 271

Another meal that could be considered on the "no-fly" list for a diet, thanks to its trademark creamy sauce, Chicken a la King gets cleaned up and its calories condensed in this mouthwatering makeover. To lower the calorie count, only dredge half the pieces in flour.

Makes 4-6 Servings

Ingredients
2 tablespoons olive oil, divided
1½ pounds chicken breast, skinless and boneless
½ cup, plus 1 teaspoon all-purpose flour
10 ounces baby bella mushrooms, sliced
1 large red bell pepper, diced
¾ teaspoon salt
1 cup dry vermouth
1 cup reduced-sodium chicken broth
1 cup low-fat milk
1 teaspoon butter

Directions
Step 1: Trim the chicken breast of all excess fat and cut into cubes about an inch big.

Step 2: Heat 1 tablespoon oil in a large skillet over medium-high heat. While the oil is heating, toss chicken with the flour in a medium bowl until coated. When the oil is hot, add the chicken to the skillet and cook until it starts to brown, about 2 to 4 minutes. Remove from skillet with a slotted spoon and set aside.

Step 3: Add the rest of the olive oil to the skillet, followed by the mushrooms and the diced red pepper. Sauté until the pepper softens and the mushrooms begin to brown and lose their water, about 5 to 6 minutes.

Step 4: Now add the vermouth to the pan, scraping up any brown bits while the vermouth comes to a boil. Gently whisk in the milk and broth.

Continued . . .

Step 5: Crush the butter into the remaining flour until you make a paste. Lower the heat in the pan and add the paste. Mash into the mixture until it begins to thicken.

Step 6: Return chicken to the pan and toss into the mixture. Cook on low heat an additional 7-10 minutes, until the chicken is cooked completely through.

Nutritional Information

Calories 271		Total Carbohydrates 10.2 g	3%
Calories from Fat 98		Dietary Fiber 1.4 g	6%
	% Daily Value	Sugars 5.9 g	
Total Fat 10.9 g	17%	Protein 30.4 g	
Saturated Fat 1.5 g	8%	Vitamin A	20%
Trans Fat		Vitamin C	64%
Cholesterol 67mg	22%	Calcium	9%
Sodium 520mg	22%	Iron	19%

"Sancerrely" Yours Chicken

Total Calories Per Serving: 290

Another way to enjoy the flavor of liquor on a fast day without actually indulging in it—or the extra empty calories that come along with imbibing.

Makes 4 Servings

Ingredients

4 chicken breasts, skinless and
boneless
2 tablespoons flour
¼ teaspoon salt
¼ teaspoon paprika
¼ teaspoon ground black
pepper

1 tablespoon olive oil
½ cup chicken broth
½ cup dry Sancerre (or other
dry white wine)
2 teaspoons parmesan cheese,
grated

Directions

Step 1: Preheat oven to 350° and trim chicken of excess fat. Set aside.

Step 2: Combine the flour, paprika, salt, and pepper in a shallow dish. Dredge the chicken in the flour mixture.

Step 3: Heat the olive oil over high heat in an ovenproof skillet. Add chicken and sear about 2 minutes per side. Now add the chicken broth and wine to the pan and bring to a boil.

Step 4: Once the liquid boils, remove the pan from heat. Tent with a sheet, or several sheets, of aluminum foil and bake chicken for 30 minutes, until chicken is cooked all the way through.

Step 5: Remove chicken from oven and sprinkle with cheese. Serve.

Nutritional Information

Calories 290		Sodium 342mg	14%
Calories from Fat 109		Total Carbohydrates 4g	1%
	% Daily Value	Protein 33.9g	
Total Fat 12.1g	19%	Vitamin A	3%
Saturated Fat 2.9g	14%	Vitamin C	0%
Trans Fat		Calcium	2%
Cholesterol 101mg	34%	Iron	10%

Pecan-Chipotle Chicken Fingers

Total Calories Per Serving: 269

You will go *nuts* for this low-cal chicken recipe! (Uh, sorry.) The pecans are packed with nutrients and antioxidants, and have also actually been shown help lower cholesterol.

Makes 4 Servings

Ingredients
　　Cooking spray
　　4 boneless, skinless chicken breasts
　　1 egg
　　½ cup pecan halves
　　¼ cup plain dry breadcrumbs
　　1½ teaspoons freshly grated orange zest
　　½ teaspoon salt
　　¼ teaspoon ground chipotle pepper

Directions
Step 1: Preheat oven to 350°. Trim chicken of excess fat and slice into "fingers"—about 3-4 per breast.

Step 2: Whisk the egg in a bowl. In a food processor, combine the pecans, ground chipotle pepper, breadcrumbs, and orange zest, pulsing until the pecans are finely ground. Remove from food processor and pour mixture into a shallow baking dish.

Step 3: Dip each piece of chicken in the whisked egg and then dredge in the pecan-chipotle mixture and move each to the baking dish.

Step 4: Bake chicken at 350° for 25-30 minutes, until cooked all the way through. Serve immediately. Serve with a large green salad, if desired.

Nutritional Information

Calories 269		Total Carbohydrates 4.6 g	2%
Calories from Fat 144		Dietary Fiber 1.1 g	4%
	% Daily Value	Sugars 0.7 g	
Total Fat 14.5 g	22%	Protein 29.5 g	
Saturated Fat 2.8 g	14%	Vitamin A	2%
Trans Fat		Vitamin C	1%
Cholesterol 114mg	38%	Calcium	3%
Sodium 319mg	13%	Iron	10%

Boneless Buffalo Wings

Total Calories Per Serving: 244

Here's a treat that would go nicely over a small green salad—complete with chopped celery, shaved carrots, and a dollop of make-it-yourself creamy blue cheese dressing!

Makes 10 Servings

Ingredients

- 3 tablespoons nonfat buttermilk
- 3 tablespoons Frank's hot sauce
- 3 tablespoons distilled white vinegar
- ½ teaspoon cayenne pepper
- 2 pounds chicken tenders
- 6 tablespoons whole-wheat flour
- 6 tablespoons cornmeal
- Cooking spray
- 4 ounces reduced-fat sour cream
- 4 ounces crumbled blue cheese
- 1 teaspoon cayenne pepper

Directions

Step 1: In a large bowl, combine the buttermilk, hot sauce, vinegar, and half a teaspoon of cayenne pepper. Whisk together and add chicken. Cover and marinate for at least one hour.

Step 2: While the chicken is marinating, and in another smaller bowl, whisk together the sour cream, crumbled blue cheese, and another teaspoon of cayenne pepper. Cover and refrigerate.

Step 3: In a medium sized bowl, mix together the whole-wheat flour and cornmeal. Remove the chicken pieces from the marinade and place on a separate plate. Save the marinade.

Step 4: Dredge each chicken piece in the flour and cornmeal mixture, then dunk in reserved marinade.

Step 5: Heat a large grill pan to medium high heat and coat with cooking spray. Place the chicken tenders in the pan and grill about 6 to 8 minutes per side. Remove from pan and serve with the creamy blue cheese mixture.

Nutritional Information

Calories 244		Total Carbohydrates 16.7 g	6%
Calories from Fat 75		Dietary Fiber 1.6 g	6%
	% Daily Value	Sugars 4.8 g	
Total Fat 8.4 g	13%	Protein 25.5 g	
Saturated Fat 3.5 g	17%	Vitamin A	6%
Trans Fat		Vitamin C	1%
Cholesterol 57mg	19%	Calcium	19%
Sodium 637mg	27%	Iron	3%

Basic Baked Pesto Chicken

Total Calories Per Serving: 289

Plain baked chicken gets a new lease on flavor with just a hint of pesto and some sliced tomatoes for color and vitamins!

Makes 4 Servings

Ingredients
4 boneless skinless chicken breast halves
½ cup pesto (see page 45)
2 plum tomatoes, sliced
½ cup part-skim mozzarella cheese, shredded

Directions
Step 1: Preheat oven to 350°. Trim chicken of all extra fat.

Step 2: Place chicken pieces in an ovenproof glass casserole dish, or similar. Spoon pesto onto each piece of chicken and smooth over the top.

Step 3: Bake chicken for 25 to 30 minutes, until it's cooked through. Remove chicken from oven but leave oven on.

Step 4: On top of each piece of chicken, place sliced tomato and a large pinch of cheese. Return to oven and bake about 3 to 5 minutes longer, until the cheese melts. Remove from oven and serve.

Nutritional Information

Calories 289		Total Carbohydrates 4.4 g	1%
Calories from Fat 109		Dietary Fiber 0.9 g	4%
	% Daily Value	Sugars 3.5 g	
Total Fat 12.1 g	19%	Protein 40.5 g	
Saturated Fat 2.2 g	11%	Vitamin A	11%
Trans Fat		Vitamin C	24%
Cholesterol 105mg	35%	Calcium	13%
Sodium 590mg	25%	Iron	10%

Turkey Chili

Total Calories Per Serving: 222

A yummy alternative to Chili con Carne, this low-calorie chili will not only be a satisfying dinner solution on a fast day, it will also be a hit at your next Superbowl party. On non-fast days, part-skim mozzarella cheese and nonfat sour cream nicely complement this chili.

Makes 8 servings

Ingredients

1 pound lean ground turkey or chicken

1 medium jalapeño, finely chopped

2 cloves garlic, finely chopped

28 ounces canned tomatoes, undrained

8 ounces pinto beans, drained, rinsed

1 cup water

1 cup sweet corn

2 tablespoons chili powder

2 teaspoons ground cumin

1 teaspoon dried oregano

Directions

Step 1: Heat a large stock pot or dutch oven over medium-high heat. When the pot is hot, add ground turkey and brown, about 5 to 7 minutes.

Step 2: When the turkey browns, toss in jalapeños and garlic and sauté.

Step 3: After about 3 to 5 minutes, add the rest of the ingredients. Heat the chili to a boil, then reduce heat to low. Cover and simmer 30 to 45 minutes, stirring occasionally. Serve and enjoy.

Nutritional Information

Calories 222		Total Carbohydrates 26.9 g	9%
Calories from Fat 44		Dietary Fiber 6.3 g	25%
	% Daily Value	Sugars 3.9 g	
Total Fat 4.9 g	8%	Protein 19.2 g	
Saturated Fat 1.4 g	7%	Vitamin A	1%
Trans Fat		Vitamin C	42%
Cholesterol 40mg	13%	Calcium	5%
Sodium 53mg	2%	Iron	27%

Asian-Inspired Turkey

Total Calories Per Serving: 200

One doesn't usually think of turkey in Asian cuisine, but as an alternative to chicken or red meat, it actually holds its own in many kinds of dishes. Here, dark meat turkey becomes the protein foundation for wonderful vegetables typically found in Asian dishes, like bamboo shoots, bok choy, Chinese cabbage, and baby corn.

Makes 8 Servings

Ingredients

4 boneless turkey thighs, sliced into slivers
1 teaspoon five-spice powder
½ teaspoon freshly ground black pepper
8 ounces shiitake mushrooms, sliced
1 cup red bell pepper, sliced into slivers
5 leaves baby bok choy, quartered lengthwise
15 ounces baby corn
8 ounces bamboo shoots, sliced
2 tablespoons hoisin sauce
2 tablespoons oyster sauce
1 tablespoon low-sodium soy sauce
2 teaspoons fresh ginger, grated
2 teaspoons dark sesame oil
3 garlic cloves, minced
1 tablespoon canola oil
2 cups Chinese cabbage, sliced thin
½ cup scallions, chopped

Directions

Step 1: Heat canola oil in a large nonstick skillet over medium-high heat. Add sesame oil to pan; swirl to coat. Sprinkle turkey with five-spice powder and black pepper. Add to pan and cook 3 minutes on each side until browned. Remove turkey from pan with a slotted spoon and set aside.

Step 2: Add to the pan: the shiitake mushrooms, red pepper, bok choy, baby corn, and bamboo shoots and sauté 3 to 5 minutes.

Step 3: In a small bowl, whisk together the hoisin sauce, oyster sauce, low-sodium soy sauce, ginger, and garlic. Add to the skillet and bring to a boil. When mixture boils, lower the heat and simmer, covered, about 5 minutes.

Step 4: Add the turkey and toss well with the vegetables and sauce. Continue to simmer another 8 to 10 minutes to get flavors to meld, stirring in the cabbage and scallions during the last 2 minutes. Serve and enjoy.

Nutritional Information

	% Daily Value		
Calories 200		Total Carbohydrates 17.5 g	6%
Calories from Fat 87		Dietary Fiber 3.8 g	15%
		Sugars 5 g	
Total Fat 9.7 g	15%	Protein 13.3 g	
Saturated Fat		Vitamin A	32%
Trans Fat		Vitamin C	54%
Cholesterol	0%	Calcium	4%
Sodium 177mg	7%	Iron	15%

Simmering Steak Fajitas

Total Calories Per Serving: 230

Making steak fajitas in a slow cooker is a breeze. As an added benefit, the slow cooker renders the beef moist and tender and combines the flavors of all the ingredients in a way that can't be done with a skillet or grill.

Makes 12 Fajitas, or 6 to 8 Servingss

Ingredients

Cooking spray

1 cup chunky salsa

2 cloves garlic, finely chopped

1 ½ teaspoons chipotle chili pepper powder

½ teaspoon salt

½ teaspoon ground cumin

18 ounces beef flank steak, fat trimmed

1 sweet onion, cut into ¾-inch wedges

1 red bell pepper, cut into ¾-inch strips

1 medium yellow bell pepper, cut into ¾-inch strips

12 low-fat flour toruntilas (8 inch)

Fat-free sour cream, if desired

Directions

Step 1: Spray 3- to 4-quart slow cooker with cooking spray. Add salsa, garlic, chili pepper powder, salt, and cumin to cooker.

Step 2: Now slice meat into strips. Stir into other ingredients and cover. Cook on lowest setting for 7 hours.

Step 3: After 7 hours, uncover slow cooker and add onion and bell peppers, and increase heat to high. Cover and cook an additional 30 to 45 minutes.

Step 4: Right before serving, heat toruntilas in microwave for 1 to 2 minutes, or coat a medium skillet with cooking spray, heat on high, and warm the toruntilas for about 30 seconds per side.

Step 5: Spoon about ½ cup beef mixture down center of each warm toruntila and top with sour cream, if desired. Fold over and serve.

Nutritional Information

Calories 230		Total Carbohydrates 22.7 g	8%
Calories from Fat 47		Dietary Fiber 3.7 g	15%
	% *Daily Value*	Sugars 3.6 g	
Total Fat 5.2 g	8%	Protein 22.7 g	
Saturated Fat 1.7 g	8%	Vitamin A	22%
Trans Fat		Vitamin C	67%
Cholesterol 58mg	19%	Calcium	5%
Sodium 408mg	17%	Iron	71%

Slow-Cooked Red Curry Beef

Total Calories Per Serving: 249

In an exciting take on traditional spicy Thai red curry, slow cooking combines all the flavors just right. For a more authentic experience, on a non-fast day, serve over jasmine rice.

Makes 8 servings

Ingredients

14 ounces stewing beef, trimmed of all fat
⅛ teaspoon salt
1 red onion, finely chopped
4 garlic cloves, minced
¾ cup low-fat, reduced-sodium beef broth
1 tablespoon dark brown sugar

3 tablespoons red curry paste
2 tablespoons fish sauce or soy sauce
2 tablespoons lime juice
12 ounces light coconut milk
1 jalapeño pepper, minced
2 cups baby spinach

Directions

Step 1: Heat a large stock pot or dutch oven over medium-high heat. Add beef and brown for about 5 minutes. Remove from pot with a slotted spoon and set aside, leaving pan drippings.

Step 2: Add onion and garlic to the pot and sauté 5 minutes, or until onions are tender and slightly translucent.

Step 3: Add beef broth, brown sugar, curry paste, fish sauce, lime juice, coconut milk, and pepper and bring to a boil. Return beef and all juices to the pot and reduce heat to simmer. Simmer meat on low for 2 and a half to 3 hours.

Step 4: Uncover pot and stir in spinach. Cover and cook on low again for an additional 15 minutes. Serve warm.

Nutritional Information

Calories 249		Total Carbohydrates 8.9 g	3%
Calories from Fat 146		Dietary Fiber 1.8 g	7%
	% Daily Value	Sugars 4.1 g	
Total Fat 16.2 g	25%	Protein 17.2 g	
Saturated Fat 11.8 g	59%	Vitamin A	16%
Trans Fat		Vitamin C	13%
Cholesterol 44mg	15%	Calcium	2%
Sodium 724mg	30%	Iron	60%

Tex-Mex Steak with Tasty Tomauntilo Sauce

Total Calories Per Serving: 255

Here's a recipe giving a simple grilled skirt steak a little extra zing. It can also work with other cuts of beef, so don't be afraid to experiment.

Makes 4 Servings

Ingredients
1 guajillo chili, stemmed
3 tablespoons chopped fresh oregano
2 tablespoons fresh lime juice
1 tablespoon olive oil
1½ teaspoons ground cumin
8 garlic cloves, minced
12 ounces skirt steak, trimmed
½ cup sliced onion
8 ounces tomauntilos, husks removed
Cooking spray
Salt and pepper
2 tablespoons chopped fresh cilantro

Directions
Step 1: Finely chop the chili, then combine with 1 tablespoon of the oregano, 1 tablespoon of the lime juice, the olive oil, 1 teaspoon cumin, and half the minced garlic. Place the steak in the marinade and toss to coat. Cover and leave out for 1 hour, or cover and refrigerate for up to overnight.

Step 2: If steak has been refrigerated, pull out of refrigerator and let stand at least one hour prior to cooking. Preheat oven to 450°.

Step 3: On a baking sheet coated with cooking spray, spread out the remaining garlic, onion, and tomauntilos in a single layer and bake for 20 minutes or until charred. Remove from oven and let stand. Turn off oven.

Step 4: In a bowl, combine cooled tomauntilo mixture, remaining 2 tablespoons oregano, remaining 1 tablespoon of lime juice, remaining cumin, plus salt and pepper in a blender. Process until smooth. Pour into a bowl and set aside.

Step 5: Heat a grill pan on high heat and coat with cooking spray. Grill steak 5 minutes per side for medium rare. Slice steak and plate on a serving platter. Drizzle with sauce and sprinkle with cilantro.

Nutritional Information

Calories 255		Total Carbohydrates 10.2 g	3%
Calories from Fat 120		Dietary Fiber 3.2 g	13%
	% Daily Value	Sugars 1.1 g	
Total Fat 13.4 g	21%	Protein 24.3 g	
Saturated Fat 3.9 g	20%	Vitamin A	7%
Trans Fat		Vitamin C	24%
Cholesterol 50 g	17%	Calcium	9%
Sodium 652mg	27%	Iron	28%

Asian-Inspired Surf-n-Turf

Total Calories Per Serving: 260

A delicious guilt-free way to get that Chinese food fix! Don't panic if you don't have all the ingredients for this one on hand. You can always substitute dry sherry for the sake (rice wine), and soy sauce for the oyster sauce, without changing the calorie count significantly.

Makes 6 Servings

Ingredients

¼ cup sake
1½ tablespoons oyster sauce
2 teaspoons cornstarch
4 teaspoons peanut oil
12 ounces steak, thinly sliced
1 teaspoon crushed red pepper

16 ounces small shrimp, peeled, deveined, and chopped
1 pound bok choy, sliced into 1-inch pieces

Directions

Step 1: In a small bowl, dissolve cornstarch in sake and oyster sauce using a wire whisk. Set aside.

Step 2: In a large nonstick skillet, heat half the peanut oil. Add beef and crushed red pepper, and sauté until beef begins to brown, for about 3 to 4 minutes.

Step 3: Keeping the beef and its juices in the pan, next add the shrimp until the shrimp turns pink and opaque, approximately 2 to 3 minutes. Pour beef and shrimp into a bowl, with all the juices, and set aside. Place skillet back on heat.

Step 4: Add the rest of the peanut oil to the skillet and toss in the bok choy and cook, stirring, until it begins to wilt.

Step 5: Now return the beef-shrimp mixture and all the juices to the pan and continue to cook. Stir in the cornstarch mixture and continue stirring until the sauce begins to thicken.

Step 6: Remove from heat and serve.

Nutritional Information

	% Daily Value		
Calories 260		Total Carbohydrates 3.8 g	1%
Calories from Fat 60		Dietary Fiber 0.8 g	3%
		Sugars 2.2 g	
Total Fat 6.7 g	10%	Protein 34.8 g	
Saturated Fat 1.5 g	8%	Vitamin A	68%
Trans Fat		Vitamin C	57%
Cholesterol 243mg	81%	Calcium	13%
Sodium 605mg	25%	Iron	16%

Pork Gets Plummed!

Total Calories Per Serving: 283

Pork is a meat that combines nicely with sweet fruit, and pork loin is a surprisingly lean and low-calorie cut of meat, all things considered. For this recipe, a pork loin is combined with ripe plums and slow cooked to yield a dish that is as sweet as it is savory.

Makes 4-6 servings

Ingredients

1 tablespoon ground cinnamon
1 tablespoon ground allspice
24 ounces pork tenderloin, trimmed
Cooking spray
10 ounces of jarred plum sauce
½ cup water
2 plums, pitted and sliced

Directions

Step 1: In a small bowl, toss the ground cinnamon together with the allspice.

Step 2: Rinse the pork and pat dry. Trim all excess fat. Now rub the cinnamon and allspice mixture into the pork.

Step 3: Coat an electric slow cooker with cooking spray. Place spice-rubbed pork in the slow cooker, and cover with the plum sauce.

Step 4: Add the water and plum wedges to the cooker and cover. Cook on high for 4 hours, or until the pork is tender. Plate and serve with the delicious sauce.

Nutritional Information

Calories 283	Total Carbohydrates 10.0 g	9%
Calories from Fat 58	Dietary Fiber 2.1 g	5%
% Daily Value	Sugars 6.6 g	
Total Fat 6.4 g	7%	Protein 45.1 g	
Saturated Fat 2.1 g	7%	Vitamin A	5%
Trans Fat 0.1 g	Vitamin C	12%
Cholesterol 124mg	Calcium	4%
Sodium 99mg	28%	Iron	13%

Pork "Steaks" with Roasted Vegetable Medley

Total Calories Per Serving: 213

A new twist on eating steak—with much fewer calories! Enjoy pork steaks with a yummy side of summer vegetables and still keep those calories down, down, down!

Makes 4 Servings

Ingredients

Cooking spray

3 medium tomatoes, cored and sliced on the horizontal

1 zucchini, sliced into disks

1 yellow squash, sliced into disks

1 red onion, halved

3 tablespoons fresh lime juice

1 tablespoon olive oil

1 clove garlic, minced

Salt and pepper

1 16-ounce pork tenderloin, trimmed of fat and sliced into "steaks"

Directions

Step 1: Preheat oven to 475°.

Step 2: Coat a large ovenproof glass casserole dish with cooking spray and add tomatoes, zucchini, squash, and onion to the dish. Roast at 475° for 15-17 minutes, tossing occasionally.

Step 3: While the vegetables are roasting whisk together lime juice, oil, garlic, and salt and pepper in a small bowl. Set aside.

Step 4: Remove roasted veggies from oven and spoon into a bowl, then allow to cool about 20 minutes. When cool, gently toss them with the dressing.

Step 5: Heat a large nonstick skillet over medium-high heat and coat with cooking spray. Season pork steaks with salt and pepper and sear about 4 minutes per side.

Step 6: Remove pork from heat, let stand 10 minutes, and plate with roasted vegetables.

Nutritional Information

Calories 213		Total Carbohydrates 5 g	2%
Calories from Fat 69		Dietary Fiber 1.3 g	5%
	% Daily Value	Sugars 2.6 g	
Total Fat 7.7 g	12%	Protein 30.6 g	
Saturated Fat 1.9 g	9%	Vitamin A	3%
Trans Fat		Vitamin C	40%
Cholesterol 83mg	28%	Calcium	1%
Sodium 304mg	13%	Iron	16%

Mediterranean-Style Stuffed Pork Chops

Total Calories Per Serving: 288

Here's a great way to get an entire meal on one plate—and keep it under 300 calories while you're at it!

Makes 4 servings

Ingredients

Cooking spray
4 garlic cloves, minced
5 sun-dried tomatoes, packed without oil, diced
Salt and pepper
1 10 ounce package frozen chopped spinach, thawed, drained, and squeezed dry
¼ cup (1 ounce) crumbled reduced-fat feta cheese
½ teaspoon grated lemon rind
4 (4-ounce) boneless center-cut loin pork chops, trimmed
2 tablespoons fresh lemon juice
2 teaspoons Dijon mustard
¼ teaspoon dried oregano

Directions:

Step 1: Preheat oven to 425°. Coat a large ovenproof glass casserole dish with cooking spray and set aside.

Step 2: Heat a large nonstick skillet over medium-high heat and coat with cooking spray. Add 2 minced cloves of garlic and sauté quickly, for about a minute. Add the sun-dried tomatoes to the pan and then add the spinach, the feta, and the lemon rind. Season with salt and pepper and toss all to coat. Remove from heat and set aside to cool slightly.

Step 3: Rinse and pat-dry the pork chops. Cut a horizontal slit through thickest portion of each pork chop to form a pocket. Using a teaspoon, scoop up spinach mixture and stuff each pork chop until you've used up all the mixture. Place stuffed pork chops in the baking dish.

Step 4: In a small bowl, whisk together the remaining garlic with the lemon juice, dijon mustard, and oregano and brush half of this mixture over the top of the pork chops.

Continued . . .

Step 5: Bake the pork chops 6 to 8 minutes, and flip. Brush the other side with the remaining half of the mixture, return pork chops to oven and cook an additional 8 to 10 minutes.

Step 6: Remove from oven and let stand about 10 minutes before serving.

Nutritional Information

Calories 288		Total Carbohydrates 10.5 g	4%
Calories from Fat 100		Dietary Fiber 3.7 g	15%
	% Daily Value	Sugars 4.5 g	
Total Fat 11.1 g	17%	Protein 37.6 g	
Saturated Fat 3.8 g	19%	Vitamin A	139%
Trans Fat 0.1 g		Vitamin C	95%
Cholesterol 103mg	34%	Calcium	15%
Sodium 658mg	27%	Iron	31%

Nutty for Pork Chops!

Total Calories Per Serving: 285

Make a comfort food with a superfood? Why not? These plainly coated pork chops pick up the flavors of almond and bran, and don't require any "glue" to hold on the coating. Baking ensures the crumbs stick, and without adding unnecessary fats to the cooking.

Makes 4 Servings

Ingredients

⅓ cup all-bran
3 ounces whole almonds, unsalted
1 pound top loin pork chops, boneless
Cooking spray

Directions

Step 1: Preheat oven to 350°.
Step 2: Place the all-bran and almonds in a food processor and process to a chunky paste. It should look like natural peanut butter.
Step 3: Rinse the chops and pat dry. Trim off all extra fat. Now coat chops in the almond-bran mixture.
Step 4: Coat the bottom of an ovenproof glass casserole baking dish with cooking spray and gently lay the coated pork chops in the dish. Bake about 30 to 35 minutes and serve.

Nutritional Information

Calories 285		Total Carbohydrates 5.6 g	2%
Calories from Fat 165		Dietary Fiber 2.8 g	11%
	% Daily Value	Sugars 1.2 g	
Total Fat 18.3 g	28%	Protein 25.4 g	
Saturated Fat 4.5 g	23%	Vitamin A	1%
Trans Fat		Vitamin C	2%
Cholesterol 59mg	20%	Calcium	6%
Sodium 51mg	2%	Iron	9%

Snapper with Minty Cool Grilled Mango

Total Calories Per Serving: 201

Sweet and refreshing! The subtle flavor of the light yellow tail snapper is the perfect foil for a minty-grilled mango accompaniment.

Makes 6 servings

Ingredients

6 thick mango wedges
2 teaspoons olive oil
Cooking spray
¼ cup avocado, diced
1 tablespoon fresh mint, chopped
2 teaspoons fresh lemon juice

½ teaspoon salt
¼ teaspoon freshly ground black pepper, divided
4 6-ounce yellowtail snapper fillets
Mint sprigs, for garnish

Directions

Step 1: Heat grill pan on medium-high heat and coat with cooking spray.

Step 2: Lightly brush mango and onion slices with olive oil and lay in the pan. Grill 3 minutes per side, flipping gently, and remove. Set aside and cool.

Step 3: When mango and onion have cooled, dice and combine, in a medium-sized bowl, with avocado, mint, lemon juice, ¼ teaspoon salt, and ⅛ teaspoon pepper. Set aside. Wipe out the grill pan with dry paper towel and set that aside.

Step 4: Lightly brush the snapper with the rest of the olive oil and season with pepper and salt. Reheat grill pan and add snapper fillets. Grill 4-5 minutes per side, flipping gently. Fish is done when it flakes easily with a fork.

Step 5: Plate snapper fillets on a platter. Cover with grilled mango salsa and garnish with mint. Serve and enjoy.

Nutritional Information

Calories 201		Total Carbohydrates 7.1 g	2%
Calories from Fat 46		Dietary Fiber 1.4 g	6%
	% Daily Value	Sugars 5.4 g	
Total Fat 5.1 g	8%	Protein 30.1 g	
Saturated Fat		Vitamin A	9%
Trans Fat		Vitamin C	22%
Cholesterol 54mg	18%	Calcium	6%
Sodium 263mg	11%	Iron	4%

Island Salmon

Total Calories Per Serving: 193

Pineapple and cilantro are a great way to perk up run-of-the-mill roasted salmon in this colorful dish you're sure to enjoy!

Makes 4 Servings

Ingredients

Salt and pepper
4 teaspoons olive oil
4 4-ounce salmon steaks
2 slices pineapple, diced

2 sprigs cilantro, minced
1 tablespoon chopped shallots, minced

Directions

Step 1: Preheat oven to 425°. Line an ovenproof glass casserole dish with aluminum foil and set aside.

Step 2: Rinse the salmon and pat dry. Lay the steaks in the foil-covered casserole dish and season with salt and pepper. Drizzle with olive oil. Roast salmon steaks for 12 to 15 minutes.

Step 3: While salmon is roasting, toss together the pineapple, cilantro, shallots, with remaining olive oil.

Step 4: Remove the salmon from oven and transfer to a platter. Serve with the pineapple salsa.

Nutritional Information

	% Daily Value		
Calories 193		Total Carbohydrates 2.8 g	1%
Calories from Fat 112		Dietary Fiber	
		Sugars 1.9 g	
Total Fat 12.5 g	19%	Protein 16.9 g	
Saturated Fat 2.3 g	12%	Vitamin A	19%
Trans Fat		Vitamin C	12%
Cholesterol 48mg	16%	Calcium	2%
Sodium 74mg	3%	Iron	2%

Orange-Radish Salmon With Basil

Total Calories Per Serving: 237

So many flavors crackle to life in this uncomplicated salmon dish. Radishes are an amazing source of nutrition and contain little to no calories: Out of the 237 calories found in this dish, only 2 are from the radishes!

Makes 4 Servings

Ingredients

Cooking spray
8 shallots, halved
18 radishes, halved
½ tablespoon olive oil
Salt and pepper
1 sprig rosemary
1 sprig thyme
2 oranges, peeled and divided
4 5-ounce boneless salmon fillets, skin on
1 teaspoon chopped fresh mint or basil

Directions

Step 1: Preheat oven to 425°. Line a large, ovenproof glass casserole dish with aluminum foil and coat with cooking spray.

Step 2: In a bowl, toss shallots and radishes with olive oil, salt, and pepper, and add to the casserole dish in a single layer. Add the herb sprigs and roast 12 minutes.

Step 3: Remove the shallots and radishes from the oven and push them to the outer perimeter of the casserole. Place the salmon fillets in the center of the casserole, skin side down. Season with salt and pepper. Slice one of the oranges into thin slices and place over the salmon.

Step 4: Return casserole dish to oven and bake 15 to 17 minutes.

Step 5: While the salmon is baking, zest and then halve the remaining orange.

Step 6: Remove salmon from oven and discard wilted orange slices. Plate salmon fillets on a platter. Scrape up the shallot and radish mixture from the pan and toss with orange zest and mint. Serve over salmon, squeezing the juice of the halved orange over the fillets and roasted radishes and shallots.

Nutritional Information

Calories 237		Total Carbohydrates 7.7 g	3%
Calories from Fat 117		Dietary Fiber 1.7 g	7%
	% Daily Value	Sugars 6 g	
Total Fat 13	20%	Protein 21.6 g	
Saturated Fat 2.6 g	13%	Vitamin A	4%
Trans Fat		Vitamin C	64%
Cholesterol 60mg	20%	Calcium	4%
Sodium 257mg	11%	Iron	3%

Mongolian Barbecue Salmon

Total Calories Per Serving: 297

Okay, well maybe not authentic Mongolian Barbecue, but this sassy grilled salmon surely could hold its own at an Asian themed buffet.

Makes 6 Servings

Ingredients

- 2 tablespoons dark sesame oil, divided
- 3 garlic cloves, crushed
- ½-inch piece fresh ginger, peeled
- 2 tablespoons fresh lime juice
- 2 tablespoons lower-sodium soy sauce
- 2 teaspoons dark brown sugar
- 1 teaspoon chili paste
- 1½ teaspoons tomato paste
- 4 4-ounce fresh salmon fillets
- Cooking spray
- 2 cups sugar snap peas
- ½ cup grated radishes
- ¼ cup shallots, sliced thin
- 2 teaspoons rice vinegar

Directions

Step 1: Combine 1 tablespoon of the sesame oil with garlic and ginger in a food processor or blender and pulse until chopped. Continue pulsing while you add the lime juice, soy sauce, brown sugar, chili paste, and tomato paste.

Step 2: Heat a grill pan to high and coat with cooking spray. Place salmon in pan and brush the side of the fillet facing with the sauce. Grill 10 minutes then flip. Brush the other side with the remaining sauce and grill an additional 10 minutes. Remove salmon and set aside.

Step 3: In a bowl, toss together peas, radishes, and shallots. Combine vinegar and remaining 1 tablespoon oil, stirring well and drizzle over pea mixture.

Step 4: Plate salmon on a platter and top with pea mixture. Serve.

Nutritional Information

Calories 297		Total Carbohydrates 4.8 g	2%
Calories from Fat 168		Dietary Fiber 0.8 g	3%
	% Daily Value	Sugars 3 g	
Total Fat 18.7 g	29%	Protein 25.9 g	
Saturated Fat 3.5 g	18%	Vitamin A	7%
Trans Fat		Vitamin C	35%
Cholesterol 71mg	24%	Calcium	3%
Sodium 219mg	9%	Iron	5%

Orange Poached Catfish

Total Calories Per Serving: 212

Poaching fish is a great way to get a lot of flavor without a lot of calories. Catfish is a subtle white fish that comes alive in this "orange bath."

Makes 4 Servings

Ingredients

2 large oranges
1 teaspoon extra-virgin olive oil
½ teaspoon sea salt
4 4-ounce catfish fillets

Directions

Step 1: Zest both oranges and set the zest aside in a small bowl. Next, slice the oranges in half and squeeze out the juice into a separate bowl. Set aside.

Step 2: Heat the olive oil in a large nonstick skillet on medium high heat. Now add the orange juice. Heat for about a minute or two.

Step 3: Add the catfish fillets to the skillet and lower the heat to simmer. Cover and poach the catfish fillets in the orange juice for about 7 to 8 minutes.

Step 4: Remove the fish from the skillet and discard orange juice. Plate fillets on a platter and sprinkle with salt and orange zest. Serve warm.

Nutritional Information

Calories 212		Total Carbohydrates 8.4 g	3%
Calories from Fat 113		Dietary Fiber 0.6 g	3%
	% Daily Value	Sugars 1.3 g	
Total Fat 12.5 g	19%	Protein 15.5 g	
Saturated Fat 3 g	15%	Vitamin A	1%
Trans Fat 69mg		Vitamin C	13%
Cholesterol 23mg	23%	Calcium	4%
Sodium 238mg	10%	Iron	7%

Pan Roasted Fish with Tomatoes

Total Calories Per Serving: 255

A hearty, filling way to serve up a light fish like snapper. You could also sub in another light white fish if you choose, like tilapia or flounder. The calorie count will be about the same for either of those, if you prefer them to snapper.

Makes 4 Servings

Ingredients

1½ tablespoons olive oil

1½ teaspoons butter

2 cups plum tomato, chopped and seeded

1 tablespoon Dijon mustard

3 garlic cloves, minced

1½ tablespoons chopped fresh flat-leaf parsley

1 tablespoon minced fresh tarragon

¾ teaspoon kosher salt, divided

¾ teaspoon freshly ground black pepper, divided

¼ teaspoon crushed red pepper

1 tablespoon olive oil

4 4-ounce yellowtail snapper fillets, skin on

Directions

Step 1: In a medium skillet, heat olive oil and butter over medium-high heat. When the butter melts, add the tomatoes to the pan and sauté about 6 to 8 minutes, until the tomatoes start to fall apart.

Step 2: Now add the mustard and garlic to the tomatoes and raise the heat. Bring to a boil and then reduce heat to low.

Step 3: Simmer the tomatoes with the garlic and mustard about 2 minutes and then remove from heat. Then fold in the parsley, tarragon, ¼ teaspoon salt, ¼ teaspoon black pepper, and red pepper. Set aside.

Step 4: In a second skillet, heat oil over medium-high heat, until hot. While oil is heating, sprinkle the skin side of the snapper with salt and pepper and add to pan, seasoned-side down. Now season the other side with pepper and salt. Cook 3 minutes per side.

Step 5: Remove fish from pan. Plate on a serving platter and cover
with tomato sauce. Serve.

Nutritional Information

Calories 255		Total Carbohydrates 3.1 g	1%
Calories from Fat 112		Dietary Fiber 1 g	4%
	% Daily Value	Sugars	
Total Fat 12.5 g	19%	Protein 30.3 g	
Saturated Fat 1.9 g	10%	Vitamin A	8%
Trans Fat		Vitamin C	9%
Cholesterol 58 g	19%	Calcium	7%
Sodium 657mg	27%	Iron	6%

Lemony Poached Halibut

Total Calories Per Serving: 223

Light and clean tasting, this halibut will make you feel good about being on a diet and eating healthy. The flavors are so powerful here, you'll never miss the fat!

Makes 4 Servings

Ingredients

3 tablespoons olive oil

1 tablespoon grated lemon zest

1½ tablespoons fresh lemon juice

4 teaspoons chopped fresh cilantro

4 teaspoons chopped fresh parsley

6 cups water

½ teaspoon black peppercorns

2 green onions, coarsely chopped

1 parsley sprig

1 cilantro sprig

4 6-ounce halibut fillets

Directions

Step 1: In a medium bowl whisk together the olive oil, lemon zest, lemon juice, cilantro, parsley, and salt. Set aside.

Step 2: In a deep skillet, add water plus the peppercorns, green onions, parsley and cilantro sprigs. Bring to a boil.

Step 3: Reduce heat to simmer and add halibut fillets. Poach for 10 minutes and remove fish from pan with a slotted spoon. Place fillets on serving platter and pour the sauce over them before serving.

Nutritional Information

Calories 223		Total Carbohydrates 0.9 g	0%
Calories from Fat 94		Dietary Fiber	
	% Daily Value	Sugars	
Total Fat 10.4 g	16%	Protein 30.5 g	
Saturated Fat 1.5 g	8%	Vitamin A	8%
Trans Fat		Vitamin C	9%
Cholesterol 46mg	15%	Calcium	8%
Sodium 669mg	28%	Iron	8%

Sautéed Halibut with Nutty Roasted Pepper Sauce

Total Calories Per Serving: 205

Plain old halibut gets a rich, nutty kick with the addition of roasted red peppers and toasted almonds. Cooking with hazelnut oil only ups the nut quotient, so if you want to quiet it down some, opt to add in plain old olive oil instead.

Makes 4 servings

Ingredients

2 medium roasted red peppers, drained and rinsed

½ teaspoon salt, divided

1½ tablespoons slivered almonds, toasted

1 tablespoon hazelnut oil

1 tablespoon red wine vinegar

¼ teaspoon freshly ground black pepper

⅛ teaspoon ground red pepper

2 garlic cloves, chopped

4 6-ounce halibut fillets

Cooking spray

Lemon wedges, for garnish (optional)

Preparation

Step 1: In a blender or food processor, pulse together the roasted red peppers with the salt, almonds, hazelnut oil, red wine vinegar, black pepper, red pepper, and garlic. Blend until smooth. Pour into a bowl and set aside.

Step 2: Coat a large skillet with cooking spray and heat over medium-high heat.

Step 3: Rinse and pat dry the halibut fillets. Sprinkle each with a touch of salt and pepper. Add to the pan, and sprinkle the opposite sides with salt and pepper. Cook 6 minutes per side, flipping gently.

Step 4: Remove halibut fillets from the pan and place on a serving platter. Drizzle roasted red pepper and almond sauce over fillets and garnish with lemon wedges, if desired.

Nutritional Information

Calories 205		Total Carbohydrates 3.8 g	1%
Calories from Fat 60		Dietary Fiber 1.2 g	5%
	% Daily Value	Sugars 2 g	
Total Fat 6.6 g	10%	Protein 31.1 g	
Saturated Fat 0.9 g	4%	Vitamin A	29%
Trans Fat		Vitamin C	89%
Cholesterol 46mg	15%	Calcium	8%
Sodium 27mg	11%	Iron	9%

Mahi-Mahi with Tropical Salsa

Total Calories Per Serving: 264

Mahi-mahi gets a juicy and delicious boost with the addition of this spicy-sweet tropical salsa. On non-fast days, serve this dish on a bed of coconut rice and your family will be licking their plates clean!

Makes 4 to 6 Servings

Ingredients

1 pound mahi-mahi fillet
2 tablespoons low-sodium soy sauce
4 tablespoon olive oil
1 clove garlic, minced
1 mango, diced
½ papaya, diced

1 teaspoon ginger
The juice of 1 lime
The zest of 1 lime
2 tablespoons red onion, chopped
Salt and pepper

Directions

Step 1: Preheat the broiler to high.

Step 2: In a medium sized bowl, whisk together the soy sauce, 2 tablespoons of the olive oil, and the garlic.

Step 3: Rinse clean and pat dry the mahi mahi and place it in an ovenproof glass casserole dish. Pour the marinade over the fish, toss to coat, and let sit covered, about half an hour.

Step 4: While the mahi mahi marinates, add the mango, papaya, ginger, lime juice, lime zest, red onion, and salt and pepper to a bowl. Drizzle in the remaining olive oil and toss to coat. Set aside.

Step 5: Broil the mahi mahi 6 minutes per side. Remove from oven and cool 3 to 5 minutes. Set on serving platter and cover with the tropical salsa. Serve immediately.

Nutritional Information

Calories 264		Total Carbohydrates 13.6 g	5%
Calories from Fat 129		Dietary Fiber 1.8 g	7%
	% Daily Value	Sugars 10.5 g	
Total Fat 14.3 g	22%	Protein 22.2 g	
Saturated Fat 2.1 g	10%	Vitamin A	16%
Trans Fat		Vitamin C	64%
Cholesterol 40mg	13%	Calcium	12%
Sodium 538mg	22%	Iron	7%

Shrimp Pad Thai

Total Calories Per Serving: 183

Any diet that allows for noodles is my kind of diet! This filling take on pad thai is sure to delight and satisfy. (Just wait until tomorrow to go back for seconds.)

Makes 4 Servings

Ingredients
1 tablespoon rice vinegar
2½ teaspoons honey
1 tablespoon chili paste
1 tablespoon low-sodium soy sauce
12 ounces peeled and deveined medium shrimp
4 ounces uncooked flat rice noodles
1 tablespoon peanut oil
2 tablespoons cashews, chopped
1 tablespoon garlic, minced
2 teaspoons chopped peeled fresh ginger
12 sweet mini peppers, halved
¾ cup carrots, shaved
¼ teaspoon salt
¾ cup snow peas, trimmed
¾ cup fresh bean sprouts

Directions
Step 1: In a medium bowl, whisk together the vinegar, honey, chili paste, and soy sauce. Toss shrimp into mixture and evenly coat. Cover and marinate 30 minutes to an hour.

Step 2: Cook noodles according to package direction. Rinse, drain, and set aside.

Step 3: Coat a large skillet with the peanut oil. When oil is hot, add cashews, garlic, ginger, and chili to the pan. Sauté about 2 to 3 minutes, until garlic browns. Remove cashew mixture with slotted spoon and set aside.

Step 4: Turn up the heat and then add sweet peppers, carrot, and salt to the drippings in the skillet. Add shrimp with the entire marinade and cook 3 to 4 minutes.

Step 5: Now add the noodles and snow peas to the pan and cook and additional 2 minutes. Remove from heat and stir in sprouts. Let sit a minute or two and serve.

Nutritional Information

Calories 183		Total Carbohydrates 18.2 g	6%
Calories from Fat 51		Dietary Fiber 1.3 g	5%
	% Daily Value	Sugars 5.2 g	
Total Fat 5.7 g	9%	Protein 15 g	
Saturated Fat 1 g	5%	Vitamin A	7%
Trans Fat		Vitamin C	50%
Cholesterol 55mg	18%	Calcium	5%
Sodium 689mg	29%	Iron	7%

Calorie-Conscious Cajun Shrimp

Total Calories Per Serving: 171

Here's a spicy fun cajun treat that won't break the calories bank!
Serve with a large side salad or even a small portion (⅛ cup or less)
of brown rice.

Makes 4 Servings

Ingredients

1½ pounds large shrimp,
    peeled and de-veined
1 teaspoon paprika
¾ teaspoon dried thyme
¾ teaspoon dried oregano

¼ teaspoon garlic powder
¼ teaspoon salt
¼ teaspoon black pepper
¼ teaspoon cayenne pepper
1 tablespoon vegetable oil

Directions

Step 1: In a large bowl, toss together the paprika, thyme, oregano,
garlic powder, salt, pepper, and cayenne pepper.

Step 2: In a large, nonstick skillet, heat the vegetable oil over medium
high heat.

Step 3: While the oil is heating, rinse the shrimp and pat it dry. Toss
the shrimp into the spice mixture, and then toss the shrimp
into the heated oil.

Step 4: Sauté shrimp about 3 minutes per side, and remove from
heat. Serve and enjoy.

Nutritional Information

	% Daily Value			
Calories 171		Total Carbohydrates 3.9 g	1%	
Calories from Fat 3.5 g		Dietary Fiber		
	% Daily Value	Sugars		
Total Fat 3.5 g	5%	Protein 32.1 g		
Saturated Fat 0.7 g	4%	Vitamin A	5%	
Trans Fat		Vitamin C	1%	
Cholesterol 234mg	81%	Calcium	1%	
Sodium 360mg	15%	Iron	3%	

Quinoa Crusted Shrimp

Total Calories Per Serving: 232

Another healthy, tasty way to use quinoa! Traditional fried shrimp is delicious but a definite no-no even on this relaxed diet. There's no way you ever want to give up over 450 calories to a handful of those delicious breaded treats, no matter how good they are! Well, you can still enjoy the experience of fried shrimp without paying the price, thanks to our handy friend quinoa and the oven!

Makes 4-6 Servings

Ingredients

½ cup flour
Salt and pepper
½ teaspoon ground cumin
½ teaspoon paprika
¾ teaspoon garlic powder

½ teaspoon onion powder
2 eggs, beaten
1 cup raw quinoa
1 pound medium shrimp

Directions

Step 1: In a bowl, mix together the flour, salt, pepper, cumin, paprika, garlic powder, and onion powder. Set aside. In a separate bowl, whisk together the eggs. Set aside. In another bowl, add the quinoa.

Step 2: Preheat oven to 425°. Coat a large glass ovenproof casserole dish with cooking spray. Using tongs, dredge each shrimp into the spiced flour, then dunk in the egg batter, then roll in the quinoa.

Step 3: Place the shrimp in a single layer in the casserole dish and bake 15 minutes, or until the shrimp is cooked all the way through. Serve.

Nutritional Information

Calories 232		Total Carbohydrates 25.8 g	9%
Calories from Fat 37		Dietary Fiber 2.3 g	9%
	% Daily Value	Sugars	
Total Fat 4.1 g	6%	Protein 23 g	
Saturated Fat 0.7 g	3%	Vitamin A	3%
Trans Fat		Vitamin C	0%
Cholesterol 203 mg	68%	Calcium	4%
Sodium 581 mg	24%	Iron	26%

Seared Scallops with Minty Creamed Peas

Total Calories Per Serving: 267

The flavor of scallops really pops on a base of puréed minty creamed peas!

Makes 4 Servings

Ingredients

6 teaspoons olive oil
2 leeks, thinly sliced
Salt
2 cups green peas
¾ cup non-fat milk
1 teaspoon minced fresh mint
1 pound sea scallops
1 teaspoon fresh lemon juice
2 teaspoon white wine vinegar

Directions

Step 1: Heat a teaspoon of the olive oil in a large nonstick skillet on medium-low heat. When the oil is hot, add the leeks and a pinch of salt to the pan and cook until the leeks soften, about 4 to 5 minutes.

Step 2: When the leeks are soft, pour the peas and the milk into the pan. Cook an additional 5 to 6 minutes, until the peas are thoroughly cooked and soft. Add the mint in the last minute. Remove from heat and set aside to cool, about 15 to 20 minutes.

Step 3: Add pea mixture to a blender or food processor and pulse until smooth, with a slightly chunky texture. Pour into a bowl and set aside.

Step 4: Wipe out the skillet and reheat over medium heat. Add another teaspoon of the olive oil and, when hot, add the scallops to the pan in a single layer. Sear about 3 minutes per side, flipping gently. Remove and transfer scallops to a plate. Cover.

Step 5: Now, in a small bowl, whisk together the rest of the olive oil, the lemon juice, and the vinegar.

Continued . . .

Step 6: Coat the bottom of a serving platter with the pea purée. Now place the scallops on the purée and drizzle with vinaigrette. Serve.

Nutritional Information

Calories 267		Total Carbohydrates 22 g	7%
Calories from Fat 79		Dietary Fiber 4.6 g	19%
	% Daily Value	Sugars 8.3 g	
Total Fat 8.8 g	13%	Protein 25.2 g	
Saturated Fat 1.5 g	7%	Vitamin A	29%
Trans Fat		Vitamin C	64%
Cholesterol 40 g	13%	Calcium	13%
Sodium 333mg	14%	Iron	15%

Scallops with Turkey Bacon

Total Calories Per Serving: 146

Finally, one last scallop dish for you to savor and enjoy, all while keeping those calories low. Turkey bacon makes these two great tastes, scallop and bacon, something you can enjoy without guilt on a fast day—or any day.

Makes 4 Servings

Ingredients

2 teaspoons olive oil

16 sea scallops

Salt and pepper

2 slices turkey bacon

3 to 4 shallots, sliced thin

2 garlic cloves, minced

8 ounces watercress, trimmed

Directions

Step 1: Heat olive oil in a large nonstick skillet over medium-high heat.

Step 2: Rinse and pat-dry scallops. Sprinkle one side with salt and pepper. Add to the pan, seasoned side down. Sprinkle the other side and sear about 3 minutes. Gently flip and sear an additional 2 minutes and remove from pan. Set aside.

Step 3: Wipe skillet clean with a wad of dry paper toweling and place bacon in skillet. Cook until crisp and drain. Cool, and when cool to the touch, crumble into small pieces and set aside.

Step 4: Now add shallots and garlic to the bacon drippings and sauté until soft, about 3 to 4 minutes. Toss watercress into pan and wilt, about 30 seconds to a minute only.

Step 5: Pour warm watercress mixture out onto a serving platter. Top with scallops, sprinkle with turkey bacon, and serve immediately.

Nutritional Information

	% Daily Value		
Calories 146		Total Carbohydrates 4.4 g	1%
Calories from Fat 32		Dietary Fiber	
Total Fat 3.6 g	5%	Sugars	
Saturated Fat		Protein 23 g	
Trans Fat		Vitamin A	37%
Cholesterol 45mg	15%	Vitamin C	47%
Sodium 277mg	12%	Calcium	10%
		Iron	3%

Chapter 5: Sensible Sides———

Diets will tell you that for a calorie-conscious meal, you should limit yourself to a piece of meat or other protein that's no more than 3 to 4 ounces in size (some have referred to this as a "card deck"-sized portion), and plainly prepared (meaning little to no fat used in the cooking, no skin, etc.) that you will be instructed to enjoy with a large, preferably "undressed" salad or other "sensible" side.

Well, that's pretty much what this chapter is all about. Except here, you're going to find a number of "sides" you can enjoy all on their own. Remember that portion size goes a long way in determining how many calories you take in (see card deck example above). So if you want to enjoy a larger portion of meat or fish, serve yourself less of the "side."

Here, you'll find a variety of flavorful foods, some simple, some exotic and more elaborate. So, what can you pair with these sides? The following chart on page 42 lists some calorie counts for various, plainly prepared, sources of protein.

Type of Protein (4 ounces)	Calories
Scallops	100
Mussels	98
Clams	54
Shrimp	135
Tilapia	93
Flounder	133
Salmon	234
Tuna	211
Swordfish	175
Chicken Breast (Skinless)	186
Chicken Thigh (Skinless)	215
Turkey Breast (Skinless)	118
Ham	185
Pork	162
Lamb	211
Steak	226
Tofu	79

Quinoa with Black Beans and Corn

Total Calories Per Serving: 148

Quinoa is healthy and yummy, and so incredibly versatile. Here, paired with black beans and corn, it makes for a decidedly South-western side.

Makes 12 Servings

Ingredients

1 cup quinoa
2 cups low-sodium vegetable broth
½ cup frozen corn, thawed
1 cup canned black beans, drained, rinsed

1 small tomato, roughly chopped
¼ cup green onions, chopped
1 tablespoon fresh lime juice
¼ cup chopped fresh cilantro
¼ teaspoon salt

Directions

Step 1: In a medium to large stock pot, bring the vegetable broth to a boil, and cook quinoa following the package directions.

Step 2: When all the liquid is absorbed, remove from heat. Fold the beans and the corn into the quinoa, fluffing with a fork. (The heat of the quinoa will "cook" the thawed frozen corn and warm the beans.)

Step 3: Pour the steaming quinoa into a medium sized to large bowl. Add the tomato, green onions, lime juice, cilantro, and salt and mix well. Serve warm or refrigerate 2 hours as a cool summertime side.

Nutritional Information

	% Daily Value			
Calories 148		Total Carbohydrates 20.6 g	7%
Calories from Fat 16		Dietary Fiber 3.8 g	15%
		Sugars 0.8 g	
Total Fat 1.8 g	3%	Protein 12.5 g	
Saturated Fat		Vitamin A	2%
Trans Fat		Vitamin C	9%
Cholesterol 18mg	6%	Calcium	5%
Sodium 68mg	3%	Iron	17%

Roasted Cauliflower

Total Calories Per Serving: 66

A wonderful, low-calorie alternative to roasted white potatoes. The parmesan cheese and lemon add a special zip to the subtle natural flavor of the cauliflower.

Makes 4-6 servings

Ingredients
- 1 head cauliflower
- 2 cloves of garlic, minced
- 2 tablespoons olive oil
- 1 tablespoon of lemon juice
- 2 tablespoons parmesan cheese, shredded

Directions
Step 1: Preheat oven to 400°. Chop the cauliflower into florets.

Step 2: Toss florets with the olive oil, lemon juice and garlic, and place in a glass ovenproof casserole dish or similar.

Step 3: Roast uncovered 25-30 minutes, until the florets slightly brown. Remove from oven and top with shredded parmesan. Serve and enjoy.

Nutritional Information

Calories 66		Total Carbohydrates 3.4 g	1%
Calories from Fat 46		Dietary Fiber 1.3 g	5%
	% Daily Value	Sugars 0.9 g	
Total Fat 5.1 g	8%	Protein 3.2 g	
Saturated Fat 1.5 g	8%	Vitamin A	1%
Trans Fat		Vitamin C	28%
Cholesterol 5mg	2%	Calcium	8%
Sodium 150mg	6%	Iron	3%

Roasted Veggies

Total Calories Per Serving: 80

Eggplant, squash, and zucchini were made to go together. Prepared simply, with a little olive oil and Herbs de Provence, this combination holds its own, on its own. Enjoy as an accompaniment to a lean piece of meat, or toss over pasta or rice to make a deliciously satisfying vegetarian meal.

Makes 8 Servings

Ingredients
1 large eggplant, peeled and cut into chunks
2 zucchini, sliced
2 yellow squash, sliced
2 tablespoons extra virgin olive oil
1 tablespoon Herbs de Provence
Salt and pepper, to taste

Directions
Step 1: Preheat oven to 425°.

Step 2: Add eggplant, zucchini, and squash to an ovenproof glass casserole dish, or similar, and drizzle with olive oil. Sprinkle with Herbs de Provence, salt, and pepper, and toss to coat.

Step 3: Roast mixture in middle to top of oven for 20-25 minutes, tossing occasionally. Remove from oven and serve.

Nutritional Information

Calories 80		Total Carbohydrates 8.8 g	3%
Calories from Fat 46		Dietary Fiber 4.1 g	16%
	% Daily Value	Sugars 4.0	
Total Fat 5.1 g	8%	Protein 2.3 g	
Saturated Fat 0.7 g	4%	Vitamin A	5%
Trans Fat		Vitamin C	42%
Cholesterol	0%	Calcium	2%
Sodium 15mg	1%	Iron	8%

Lemon Dijon Pasta

Total Calories Per Serving: 135

Served hot or cold, this savory side combines lemon with the zing of dijon. Keeping the haricot vert (thin, French-style string beans) raw gives this side an unexpected but delightful crunch.

Makes 4-6 Servings

Ingredients
>   8 ounces pasta (rotini or penne work best)
>   8 ounces haricot vert, roughly chopped
>   2 tablespoons olive oil
>   1 teaspoon Dijon mustard
>   2 cloves garlic, minced
>   The zest of 1 lemon
>   The juice of same lemon
>   2 ounces Parmesan cheese, shaved

Directions
Step 1: Cook pasta in a large stock pot according to package directions. Drain and rinse and pour into a large bowl, tossing with haricot vert.

Step 2: In a separate small bowl, whisk together the olive oil, dijon mustard, garlic, lemon juice, and lemon zest. Toss with pasta.

Step 3: Shave parmesan into pasta. Toss lightly together and serve.

Nutritional Information

Calories 135		Total Carbohydrates 14.6mg	5%
Calories from Fat 64		Dietary Fiber 3.4 g	14%
	% Daily Value	Sugars 1.2 g	
Total Fat 7.1 g	11%	Protein 6.1 g	
Saturated Fat 2.1 g	10%	Vitamin A	10%
Trans Fat		Vitamin C	21%
Cholesterol 7mg	2%	Calcium	12%
Sodium 147mg	6%	Iron	6%

Spinach and Feta Orzo

Total Calories Per Serving: 200

An easy side that combines two in one—a starch and a green in one tasty combo. This recipe calls for frozen spinach because it's convenient, and there are no quantity surprises when it cooks. (As much cooking as I do, I'm always shocked by how much spinach "shrinks" when it cooks!) But using fresh spinach would also make for a delicious dish here.

Makes 4-6 Servings

Ingredients
> 1 cup orzo
> 1 tablespoon olive oil
> 1 shallot, chopped
> 1 package frozen spinach, thawed and drained
> ⅓ cup feta cheese

Directions
Step 1: Cook orzo following package directions. Drain and set aside.

Step 2: While orzo is cooking, heat the olive oil in a large skillet over medium heat. Add the shallot and sauté until browned, about 3-4 minutes.

Step 3: Add the thawed, drained spinach to the skillet and cook an additional 3-5 minutes. Fold in the feta cheese, toss, and serve immediately.

Nutritional Information

Calories 200		Total Carbohydrates 27.4 g	9%
Calories from Fat 63		Dietary Fiber 2.7 g	11%
	% Daily Value	Sugars 2.5 g	
Total Fat 7 g	11%	Protein 7.8 g	
Saturated Fat 2.4 g	12%	Vitamin A	135%
Trans Fat		Vitamin C	34%
Cholesterol 11mg	4%	Calcium	13%
Sodium 196mg	8%	Iron	17%

Orzo With Veggies and White Beans

Total Calories Per Serving: 173

Packed with flavor and nutrition, you can cut the calorie count of this side by cutting down on the amount of beans used or even eliminating them altogether. (There are 76 calories in 8 ounces of cannellini beans. Cut that in half and your recipe will come in around 140 calories instead.)

Makes 8 Servings

Ingredients

1 cup orzo
2 tablespoons of olive oil
½ onion, chopped
3 cloves of garlic, minced
1 red bell pepper, chopped

1 cup mushrooms, sliced
2 cups baby spinach
8 ounces of cannellini beans, drained and rinsed
¼ cup parmesan cheese, grated

Directions

Step 1: Cook orzo according to package directions. Drain and rinse.

Step 2: While orzo is cooking, add the olive oil to a large skillet and heat over medium heat. Add onions and sauté 3-4 minutes; then garlic and sauté an additional 2 minutes. Add mushroom and sauté until the mushrooms brown slightly and loose their water. Add red pepper and continue to sauté an additional 2-4 minutes.

Step 3: Add spinach to the skillet, and fold it in with the other ingredients. When spinach begins to wilt, turn heat to low and add beans and drained orzo to the mix. Add the parmesan cheese and lightly toss. Serve warm.

Nutritional Information

Calories 173			Total Carbohydrates 29.7	10%
Calories from Fat 51			Dietary Fiber 4.4 g	18%
		% Daily Value	Sugars 2.6 g	
Total Fat 5.6 g		9%	Protein 8.2 g	
Saturated Fat 1.5 g		8%	Vitamin A	16%
Trans Fat			Vitamin C	26%
Cholesterol 5mg		2%	Calcium	11%
Sodium 130mg		5%	Iron	11%

Stuffed Peppers

Total Calories Per Serving: 182

Here's another side that's satisfying enough to be its own stand-alone dish. I happen to like red peppers, but green, orange, or yellow could also be used in this recipe.

Makes 8 Servings

Ingredients

¾ cup brown rice
Cooking spray
8 large whole red peppers
2 teaspoons olive oil

1 medium onion chopped
3 garlic cloves, minced
4 chicken sausages, out of
    casings and crumbled

Directions

Step 1: In a medium sized stock pot or rice cooker, cook rice according to package directions. Set aside.

Step 2: Preheat oven to 350. Coat a glass casserole ovenproof baking dish, or similar, with cooking spray.

Step 3: Slice the tops off the peppers and carefully scoop out gut and seeds. Place the pepper "shells" standing upright in the baking dish.

Step 4: Heat a medium skillet to high and add onion. Sauté onion 7-8 minutes, until soft. Add garlic and sauté an additional two minutes.

Step 5: Add crumbled sausage and brown, about 4-5 minutes. Then add rice and stir together with the other ingredients. Remove from heat.

Step 6: Divide the sausage and rice mixture among the standing red pepper shells, stuffing each to about ¾ to completely full. Tent with aluminum foil and bake. After 45 minutes, remove foil and continue baking and browning another 15 minutes. Let cool 10 minutes and serve.

Nutritional Information

Calories 182		Total Carbohydrates 24.9 g	8%
Calories from Fat 44		Dietary Fiber 3.8 g	15%
	% Daily Value	Sugars 5.1 g	
Total Fat 4.9 g	8%	Protein 10.9 g	
Saturated Fat 1.3 g	7%	Vitamin A	13%
Trans Fat		Vitamin C	169%
Cholesterol 28mg	9%	Calcium	5%
Sodium 593mg	25%	Iron	9%

Lemon Rosemary Beets

Total Calories Per Serving: 98

Beets are more than sweet, natural treats. They're loaded with great stuff! A wonderful source of iron, they are bursting with immunity-boosters, and they energize and revitalize you, helping your body fight against heart disease and cancer. Oh, and they're delicious, especially as prepared in this easy-peasy slow-cooker recipe.

Makes 8 Servings

Ingredients

2 pounds beets (about 6), peeled and cut into wedges
2 tablespoons fresh lemon juice
2 tablespoons extra-virgin olive oil
2 tablespoons honey
1 tablespoon cider vinegar
¾ teaspoon kosher salt
½ teaspoon freshly ground black pepper
2 rosemary sprigs
The zest of one lemon

Directions

Step 1: Place the beets, lemon juice, olive oil, honey, cider vinegar, salt, pepper, and rosemary sprigs in an electric slow cooker.
Step 2: Cover and cook on low heat for up to 8 hours.
Step 3: Remove beets from cooker and pour into bowl. Discard rosemary sprigs. Toss with lemon zest and serve.

Nutritional Information

Calories 98		Total Carbohydrates 15.8 g	5%
Calories from Fat 34		Dietary Fiber 2.3 g	9%
	% Daily Value	Sugars 13.4 g	
Total Fat 3.7 g	6%	Protein 2 g	
Saturated Fat 0.6 g	3%	Vitamin A	1%
Trans Fat		Vitamin C	10%
Cholesterol	0%	Calcium	2%
Sodium 305mg	13%	Iron	5%

Steamed Orangey Beets

Total Calories Per Serving: 72

Makes 8 Servings

Ingredients

8 medium beets
The juice of 1 orange
¼ cup packed brown sugar
1 teaspoon chopped crystallized ginger
The zest of 1 orange
Fresh chopped parsley, for garnish

Directions

Step 1: Add about an inch of water to a large stockpot or dutch oven and place a steamer basket inside. Bring the water to a boil. Add the beets, reduce heat to low, and steam for 45 minutes.

Step 2: When beets are tender, remove from heat and place in a large bowl. While they are warm, toss the beets with the orange juice, brown sugar, and ginger. Top with the orange zest and parsley and serve.

Nutritional Information

Calories 72		Dietary Fiber 2.2 g	9%
Calories from Fat 2		Sugars 14.1	
	% Daily Value	Protein 1.9 g	
Total Fat 0.2 g	0%	Vitamin A	5%
Cholesterol	0%	Vitamin C	29%
Sodium 80mg	3%	Calcium	3%
Total Carbohydrates 16.8 g	6%	Iron	5%

Yummy Carrots with Garlic, Ginger, and Lime

Total Calories Per Serving: 36

Makes 4 Servings

Ingredients

1 pound carrots, peeled and sliced into discs

1 tablespoon butter

2 garlic cloves, minced

1 teaspoon minced peeled fresh ginger

1 tablespoon chopped fresh cilantro

The zest of 1 lime

The juice of 1 lime

A pinch of salt

Directions

Step 1: Add about an inch of water to a large stockpot or dutch oven and place a steamer basket inside. Bring the water to a boil. Add the carrots, reduce heat to low, and steam for 15 minutes.

Step 2: While the carrots are cooking, melt the butter in a small skillet over medium heat. Add the garlic and ginger and sauté until the garlic just starts to brown. Remove from heat.

Step 3: When the carrots are tender, remove from heat and place in a large bowl. While they are warm, toss them with garlic-ginger-butter mix, cilantro, lime zest and lime juice. Sprinkle with salt. Serve warm.

Nutritional Information

Calories 36		Total Carbohydrates 5.4 g	15%
Calories from Fat 14		Dietary Fiber 1.7 g	51%
	% Daily Value	Sugars 2.7 g	
Total Fat 1.5 g	19%	Protein 0.5 g	
Saturated Fat 0.9 g	37%	Vitamin A	157%
Trans Fat		Vitamin C	4%
Cholesterol 4mg	10%	Calcium	2%
Sodium 128mg	23%	Iron	3%

Sweet Potato Curry

Total Calories Per Serving: 102

Here's a flavorful, satisfying curry sure to jazz up any "plainly pre-pared" piece of chicken, meat, or fish.

Makes 4 to 6 Servings

Ingredients

1 teaspoon canola oil
2 scallions, thinly sliced
2 tablespoons curry powder
1 tablespoon cumin
1 teaspoon cinnamon
10 ounces fresh spinach, washed, stemmed and coarsely chopped
2 large sweet potatoes, pre-cooked, peeled, and diced
½ cup water
1 (14 ½ ounce) can diced tomatoes
¼ cup chopped fresh cilantro

Directions

Step 1: In a large skillet, heat the oil over medium heat. Add the scallions and sauté 2-3 minutes, or until they begin to soften. When the scallions are soft, add the curry powder, cumin, and cinnamon, and stir to coat.

Step 2: Now add the tomatoes to the pan and stir in with the scallions and spices. Add the water and simmer.

Step 3: Start adding spinach a bit at a time, stirring leaves into the mixture to wilt. When all spinach has been added, simmer an additional 3-4 minutes, then stir in the sweet potato cubes.

Step 4: Cover and simmer 10 minutes. Remove from heat. Toss with cilantro and serve.

Nutritional Information

Calories 102		Total Carbohydrates 20.7 g	7%
Calories from Fat 15		Dietary Fiber 12.8 g	20%
	% Daily Value	Sugars 2.4 g	
Total Fat 1.7 g	3%	Protein 9.8 g	
Saturated Fat		Vitamin A	94%
Trans Fat		Vitamin C	84%
Cholesterol	0%	Calcium	12%
Sodium 50 g	3%	Iron	34%

Green Beans, Potatoes, and Tomatoes

Total Calories Per Serving: 76

Leave the skins on the potatoes for this dish. Not only will it give it some nice color, there are also lots of nutrients in the skins that are better in you than in the garbage chute. (Not to mention that it also saves all that peeling time.) Just make sure you scrub them clean before dicing.

Makes 6 Servings

Ingredients

1½ cups red potato, diced, unpeeled

1½ tablespoons olive oil

1 garlic clove, minced

½ cup chopped celery

½ teaspoon salt

1¼ pounds green beans, trimmed

¼ cup water

¾ pound plum tomatoes, coarsely chopped

¼ teaspoon freshly ground black pepper

Directions

Step 1: In a medium sized stock pot, bring about 4 cups of water to a boil. Add the diced red potato and continue boiling about 8-10 minutes. Drain, rinse, and set aside.

Step 2: In a large skillet, heat olive oil over medium-high heat. When oil is hot, add the garlic and sauté 1-2 minutes. Next add the potato, celery, salt, and green beans, and sauté for 3-5 minutes.

Step 3: Add the tomatoes. Reduce the heat, add ¼ cup water, cover, and simmer about 5-6 minutes, stirring occasionally. Sprinkle with pepper. Serve and enjoy.

Nutritional Information

Calories 76		Dietary Fiber 3.5 g	14%
Calories from Fat 26		Sugars 3.1 g	
	% Daily Value	Protein 2.4 g	
Total Fat 2.9 g	4%	Vitamin A	17%
Cholesterol	0%	Vitamin C	41%
Sodium 165mg	7%	Calcium	4%
Total Carbohydrates 12.1 g	4%	Iron	7%

"Pasta" from Zucchini!

Total Calories Per Serving: 84

Talk about making lemonade out of lemons! Zucchini has a such a great texture, you can use it in place of pasta in many of your favorite pasta dishes. Zucchini lasagna, zucchini and meatballs. It all comes down to the way you slice it. Literally. How does it measure up? Well, 5 ounces of pasta is about 400 calories. Five ounces of zucchini? Twenty-three.

Makes 2 Servings

Ingredients

2 zucchinis, washed and trimmed at both ends
Pinch of salt
2 tablespoons lemon juice

Directions

Step 1: Using a mandoline or a vegetable peeler, shave zucchini lengthwise into long thin strands.

Step 2: Place zucchini strands in a medium-sized bowl and toss with salt. Let stand 20 minutes.

Step 3: Rinse the zucchini strands and gently squeeze them dry. Now toss with lemon juice, more salt, and pepper.

Step 4: Add marinara sauce to your "pasta" or serve as simple side with a plainly prepared piece of meat or fish.

Nutritional Information

Calories 35		Total Carbohydrates 6.9 g	2%
Calories from Fat 0		Dietary Fiber 2.2 g	9%
	% Daily Value	Sugars 3.7 g	
Total Fat 0.5 g	1%	Protein 2.5 g	
Saturated Fat		Vitamin A	8%
Trans Fat		Vitamin C	67%
Cholesterol 0mg	0%	Calcium	3%
Sodium 100mg	4%	Iron	4%

Baked Zucchini Chips

Total Calories Per Serving: 84

Here's a side that goes with everything. And like their potato cousins, you won't be able to eat just one. Which is fine, because you don't have to worry. Even if you ate the whole plate, you'd still be hitting at just over 300 calories. (Don't eat the whole plate!)

Makes 6 Servings

Ingredients

Cooking spray

½ cup seasoned dry bread crumbs

⅛ teaspoon ground black pepper

2 ounces grated parmesan cheese

2 large egg whites

2 medium zucchini, cut into ¼-inch slices

Directions

Step 1: Preheat oven to 475°. Coat a nonstick cookie sheet with cooking spray and set aside.

Step 2: Add the breadcrumbs to a small bowl and toss with pepper and parmesan cheese. Set aside.

Step 3: In a separate bowl, whisk together the egg whites and set aside.

Step 4: Dunk the zucchini slices first in the egg whites and then roll them in the breadcrumb mixture. Place the zucchini slices on cookie sheet, in a single layer, and bake 5 minutes. When 5 minutes is up, flip the zucchini and back into the oven it goes for another 5 to 10 minutes, until brown and crispy. Serve warm.

Nutritional Information

Calories 84			Total Carbohydrates 9.5 g	3%
Calories from Fat 24			Dietary Fiber 1.2 g	5%
		% Daily Value	Sugars 1.8 g	
Total Fat 2.7 g		4%	Protein 6.4 g	
Saturated Fat 1.5 g		8%	Vitamin A	4%
Trans Fat			Vitamin C	19%
Cholesterol 7mg		2%	Calcium	11%
Sodium 287mg		12%	Iron	4%

Chapter 6: Vegetarian Options

There's a misconception that vegetarian food is less caloric than foods prepared with meats and fish. To a point, that's true, but there are many pitfalls in vegetarian cuisine that are easy to slip into.

We already talked about beans, especially chickpeas, and the mega-calories packed into them. There's also avocados, which, while bursting with nutritional qualities, including proteins and good fats, and helping you feel full, are astoundingly high in calories (360+ each!). Bananas, too, really give the calorie count a giant boost. While an orange has only 62 calories, an apple has 116, and a banana can have as many as 135 calories!

So even if you're going veggie, you still have to go into it consciously on your fast days. Pay close and careful attention to the foods you eat on your "2" days and don't think that just because it's a vegetable or fruit you're going to be okay. The recipes in this section should help you to make trimmer meal decisions.

Portobello Burgers

Total Calories Per Serving: 229

Who needs beef when you got 'bellos? These portobello burgers are bursting with flavor, and even on a bun with a slather of blue cheese, it will fall well below your calorie quotient!

Makes 4 Servings

Ingredients

Cooking spray

1½ tablespoons extra-virgin olive oil

2 cloves garlic, minced

4 large portobello mushroom caps

4 whole wheat hamburger buns

1 beefsteak tomato, sliced

2 ounces blue cheese, crumbled (½ cup)

2 cups mixed salad greens

Directions

Step 1: Heat a grill pan on medium-high and coat with cooking spray.

Step 2: Whisk the garlic into the olive oil and brush the mushroom caps with the mixture.

Step 3: Grill mushroom caps 4 to 5 minutes per side and set aside. Pour out the juices and in in the same pan, grill buns, cut sides down, for 1 to 2 minutes per side (if desired).

Step 4: Crumble blue cheese over each cap and top with a slice of tomato and about half a cup of salad greens and serve.

Nutritional Information

Calories 229		Total Carbohydrates 16.6 g	9%
Calories from Fat 152		Dietary Fiber 2.9 g	18%
	% Daily Value	Sugars 3.6 g	
Total Fat 16.9 g	18%	Protein 5.9 g	
Saturated Fat 3.8 g	19%	Vitamin A	3%
Trans Fat		Vitamin C	3%
Cholesterol 7mg	4%	Calcium	9%
Sodium 269mg	15%	Iron	6%

Cheesy Spinach Portobellos

Total Calories Per Serving: 223

Stuffed mushrooms never tasted so good! Spinach and ricotta are nicely accented here by sumptuous, salty kalamata olives, and using a part-skim ricotta keeps the calories low.

Makes 4 Servings

Ingredients

4 large portobello mushroom caps

Salt and pepper

1 cup part-skim ricotta cheese

1 cup fresh spinach, finely chopped

½ cup parmesan cheese, grated

2 tablespoons kalamata olives, pitted and chopped

Directions

Step 1: Preheat oven to 450°. Cover a medium sized cookie sheet in aluminum foil and place mushroom caps, face-up, on the pan. Season with salt and pepper and bake 20 to 25 minutes.

Step 2: While mushroom caps are baking, mix together the ricotta, spinach, ¼ cup parmesan, and olives.

Step 3: Carefully remove mushroom caps from oven. Gently clasping each with rubber tipped tongs, tip to remove excess liquid and wipe clean with a paper towel.

Step 4: Fill each cap with the ricotta-spinach mixture, sprinkle each with remaining parmesan cheese, and return to oven. Continue baking until the cheese just browns, about 8 to 10 minutes.

Nutritional Information

Calories 223		Total Carbohydrates 12.2 g	4%
Calories from Fat 106		Dietary Fiber 2.4 g	9%
	% Daily Value	Sugars 3.3 g	
Total Fat 11.8 g	18%	Protein 18.6 g	
Saturated Fat 7.2 g	36%	Vitamin A	26%
Trans Fat		Vitamin C	7%
Cholesterol 40mg	13%	Calcium	44%
Sodium 843mg	35%	Iron	7%

Simple and Savory Tomato Tart

Total Calories Per Serving: 182

This tomato tart is a filling feast, even without using a variety of heavy cheese. Serve with a green salad, and you're done!

Makes 8 Servings

Ingredients

1 reduced-fat, ready-made pie crust
2 teaspoons olive oil
½ cup shallots, finely chopped
2.5 ounces gruyere cheese, shredded
½ cup kalamata olives, pitted and chopped
3 tomatoes, cut into ½-inch-thick slices
3 tablespoons all-purpose flour
1 tablespoon cornmeal
1 tablespoon thyme
Salt and pepper
1¼ cups low-fat milk
1½ tablespoons grated parmesan cheese
3 large eggs

Directions

Step 1: Preheat oven to 350°. Remove ready-made crust from the refrigerator and let sit 10-15 minutes.

Step 2: While the crust sits, sauté the shallots in the olive oil until they begin to caramelize, about 3 to 4 minutes. Remove from heat.

Step 3: Place the crust in a pie pan and sprinkle with gruyere, caramelized shallots, and kalamata olives. Arrange half of tomato slices over the top.

Step 4: In a small bowl, mix together the flour and cornmeal and layer on top of the tomatoes. Sprinkle with thyme.

Step 5: Top the flour and cornmeal mixture with the rest of the tomato slices and season with remaining tomato slices, salt, and pepper.

Step 6: In another bowl, combine the milk, parmesan cheese, and
        eggs, and pour over the tart.
Step 7: Place pan in oven and bake for 40 minutes. Remove and let
        cool 10 minutes before serving.

Nutritional Information

Calories 182		Total Carbohydrates 12.7 g	4%
Calories from Fat 98		Dietary Fiber 1.3 g	5%
	% Daily Value	Sugars 3.5 g	
Total Fat 10.9 g	17%	Protein 9.1 g	
Saturated Fat 4.1 g	21%	Vitamin A	12%
Trans Fat		Vitamin C	18%
Cholesterol 88mg	29%	Calcium	19%
Sodium 581mg	24%	Iron	10%

Grilled and Gooey Eggplant Parmesan with Spinach

Total Calories Per Serving: 215

Forget all the frying and heavy breading. Here's a great, light way to enjoy this Italian favorite.

Makes 4 Servings

Ingredients
1 large eggplant
Cooking spray
Salt and pepper
3 tablespoons parmesan cheese, finely shredded
½ cup part-skim mozzarella cheese, shredded
2 teaspoons extra-virgin olive oil
1 tablespoon shallots, chopped
5 ounces baby spinach
1 cup crushed tomatoes
3 tablespoons fresh basil, shredded

Directions
Step 1: Preheat oven to 350°. Heat grill pan on medium-high heat and coat with cooking spray.

Step 2: Slice eggplant into ½-inch rounds and lightly season with salt and pepper. Grill eggplant until it becomes soft, about 2-3 minutes per side. Remove from heat and set aside.

Step 3: In a medium sized bowl, toss together mozzarella and parmesan cheese. Set aside.

Step 4: Heat olive oil in a medium sized skillet on medium heat. Add shallots and sauté 3-5 minutes, until slightly browned. Add spinach to the skillet by the handful. Sauté until just wilted. Remove from heat and set aside.

Step 5: Coat the bottom of a glass ovenproof casserole dish with crushed tomatoes and arrange the eggplant slices over the sauce. Onto each slice of eggplant, add a tablespoon of tomatoes, a portion of the spinach-shallot mixture, and a tablespoon of cheese. Stack and repeat as needed, until you run out of ingredients.

Step 6: Bake eggplant parmesan about 25 minutes, or until the cheese
top bubbles and slightly browns.

Nutritional Information

Calories 215		Total Carbohydrates 26.3 g	9%
Calories from Fat 73		Dietary Fiber 7.3 g	29%
	% Daily Value	Sugars 7.5 g	
Total Fat 8.1 g	12%	Protein 11.6 g	
Saturated Fat 3.4 g	17%	Vitamin A	84%
Trans Fat		Vitamin C	32%
Cholesterol 13mg	4%	Calcium	27%
Sodium 609mg	25%	Iron	24%

Kung Pao Tofu

Total Calories Per Serving: 291

No need to order out for Chinese food when you can get the same flavor and control the calories from home! This is sort of a rich treat, however, so skip the rice—unless you cut your portion in half.

Makes 4 Servings

Ingredients
1 14-ounce package extra-firm tofu, sliced into cubes
½ teaspoon Chinese five-spice powder
Cooking spray
½ cup water
3 tablespoons oyster-flavored sauce
½ teaspoon cornstarch
12 ounces broccoli florets
1 yellow bell pepper, diced
1 red bell pepper, diced
1 tablespoon minced fresh ginger
1 tablespoon minced garlic
2 tablespoons unsalted roasted peanuts
2 teaspoons hot sesame oil (optional)

Directions
Step 1: In a medium-size bowl, toss pat-dried tofu with ¼ teaspoon five-spice powder and set aside.

Step 2: In a smaller bowl, whisk together the water, oyster-flavored sauce, cornstarch, and the remaining five-spice powder.

Step 3: Coat a large nonstick skillet with cooking spray and heat over medium-high heat. Add tofu to skillet, turning regularly and cook until about 7 minutes, or until tofu browns. Remove from heat and transfer to a plate.

Step 4: To the same hot skillet, add broccoli and peppers and sauté until the veggies get soft, about 4 minutes. Add ginger and garlic and cook, stirring, until fragrant, about 30 seconds.

Step 5: Reduce heat to low. Add the oyster sauce mixture to the pan and quickly cook until the sauce thickens, not more than a minute. Return the tofu to the pan along with peanuts and stir to coat. Plate and serve immediately.

Nutritional Information

Calories 291	Total Carbohydrates 13.7 g	5%
Calories from Fat 114	Dietary Fiber 4.9 g	20%
% Daily Value	Sugars 4.7 g	
Total Fat 12.7 g 20%	Protein 12.5 g	
Saturated Fat 1.8 g 9%	Vitamin A	48%
Trans Fat	Vitamin C	255%
Cholesterol	Calcium	26%
Sodium 127mg 5%	Iron	16%

Spicy Tofu Steaks

Total Calories Per Serving: 96

Meat lovers aren't the only ones who know how to enjoy a steak. Use a basic steak rub here on these tofu treats and enjoy many of the flavors of a spicy grilled steak without the fat and worry. Serve with one of the side dishes found in the Sensible Sides chapter.

Makes 4 Servings

Ingredients
1 14-ounce package of extra-firm tofu
Peanut oil, as needed
2 tablespoons pre-made spicy steak rub

Directions
Step 1: Cut tofu lengthwise into 4 slices and pat dry with paper towel. Cut each slice in half diagonally, making 8 triangles. Set aside at room temperature for 30 minutes.

Step 2: Heat grill to medium-high and lightly cover with peanut oil. While the grill pan heats, coat the tofu with the steak rub. Grill tofu until lightly browned, about 3 to 4 minutes per side. Remove from heat and serve.

Nutritional Information

Calories 96		Total Carbohydrates 10.4 g	1%
Calories from Fat 52		Dietary Fiber 3.3 g	3%
	% Daily Value	Sugars 6.6 g	
Total Fat 5.8 g	9%	Protein 9.8 g	
Saturated Fat 0.5 g	3%	Vitamin A	46%
Trans Fat		Vitamin C	155%
Cholesterol	0%	Calcium	21%
Sodium 26		Iron	13%

Chapter 7: Low-Cal Rewards and Guilt-Free Sweets and Treats

Let's face it: We all crave some level of instant gratification. It can be hard to fight off cravings during fast days, but we stay strong because we know it will be healthy for us in the long run and that we will eventually lose weight. This chapter is here to help you reach those long term goals. No one is perfect, and we all deserve to have some sweet treats to look forward to from time to time. Every dessert in this chapter is 200 calories or less!

So keep up the hard work, and congratulate yourself for sticking to your fast! Now let's go check out your reward!

Basic Berries with Cream

Total Calories Per Serving: 99

Sweet, freshly made whipped cream is the perfect compliment to a bowl of fresh berries.

Makes 6 Servings

Ingredients

1 cup heavy cream
1 tablespoon sugar
½ cup blueberries
½ cup blackberries
½ cup strawberries
½ cup raspberries

Directions

Step 1: Using a hand mixer, whip the sugar into the heavy cream until it gets frothy and smooth.

Step 2: In a medium sized bowl, toss together all the berries. Mix well.

Step 3: Spoon out berries into bowls and top each bowl with a healthy dollop of whipped cream. Simple and delicious!

Nutritional Information

Calories 99		Total Carbohydrates 7.7 g	3%%
Calories from Fat 68		Dietary Fiber 3.3 g	3%
	% Daily Value	Sugars 5 g	
Total Fat 7.6 g	12%	Protein 0.9 g	
Saturated Fat 4.6 g	23%	Vitamin A	7%
Trans Fat		Vitamin C	24%
Cholesterol 27mg	9%	Calcium	2%
Sodium 8mg	0%	Iron	1%

Authentic Madeleine Cookies

Total Calories Per Serving: 91

What a special treat, these buttery "shells" of sweetness. Homemade with all natural ingredients, you don't have to be scared to have one or even two of these special cookies. While you need a special pan to make them, everything else about them is simple and delicious.

Makes 24 "Shells"

Ingredients

Cooking spray

2 eggs

1 cup sugar

1 cup flour, sifted

1 stick butter

1 tablespoon lemon zest

1 teaspoon vanilla extract

1 splash of brandy

Directions

Step 1: Preheat oven to 350°. Spray madeleine tins with cooking spray and set aside.

Step 2: Whisk eggs together in a small bowl and add sugar. Place the small bowl in a pot of boiling water and whisk gently over the heat, until the sugar melts. Place the butter in a microwave-safe cup and melt for 35 to 40 seconds.

Step 3: In another medium mixing bowl, sift 1 cup of flour. Add the egg and sugar mixture and stir together. Next add the butter and stir in. The batter will have a thick consistency, sort of like a loose merengue.

Step 4: Stir in the lemon zest, vanilla extract, and brandy.

Step 5: Spoon the batter into the madeleine tin. Bake 8 to 10 minutes, until the edges of the shells begin to brown. Let cool in tins about ten minutes; then remove and let cool an additional 10 minutes. Serve and enjoy.

Nutritional Information

Calories 93		Total Carbohydrates 12.4 g	4%
Calories from Fat 38		Dietary Fiber	
	% Daily Value	Sugars 8.4 g	
Total Fat 4.2 g	7%	Protein 1.1 g	
Saturated Fat 2.5 g	13%	Vitamin A	3%
Trans Fat		Vitamin C	0%
Cholesterol 24mg	8%	Calcium	0%
Sodium 32mg	1%	Iron	2%

Gingerbread Cookies

Total Calories Per Serving: 87

You don't have to wait for the holidays to enjoy the wonderful taste of gingerbread. Roll out the dough and cut into simple shapes for a spicy-sweet, low-calorie treat any day of the year.

Makes 72 Cookies

Ingredients

6 cups all-purpose flour
1 tablespoon baking powder
1 tablespoon ground ginger
1 teaspoon ground nutmeg
1 teaspoon ground cloves
1 teaspoon ground cinnamon
1 cup shortening, melted and cooled slightly
1 cup molasses
1 cup packed brown sugar
½ cup water
1 egg
1 teaspoon vanilla extract

Directions

Step 1: In a medium bowl, sift together the flour, baking powder, ginger, nutmeg, cloves, and cinnamon.

Step 2: In another bowl, add the shortening, molasses, brown sugar, water, egg, and vanilla, and mix these ingredients together until smooth.

Step 3: Pour the dry ingredients in and gradually fold all together until they mix into a dough.

Step 4: Pour out the large dough and break into three equal pieces. Pat each down to 1 ½-inch thickness, wrap individually in plastic wrap, and refrigerate at for three hours. (You may also decide to put 1 or 2 of these doughs in the freezer at this point.)

Step 5: Remove the dough from the refrigerator and preheat oven to 350°. Lightly flour a large cutting board or the like and roll out the dough to ¼ inch thickness. Cut out cookies with cutters and place them at least 1 inch apart onto an ungreased cookie sheets.

Step 6: Bake cookies about 10 to 12 minutes and remove from oven. Let sit about 10 minutes, then transfer to wire racks to cool.

Nutritional Information

Calories 87		Total Carbohydrates 13.6 g	5%
Calories from Fat 28		Dietary Fiber	
	% Daily Value	Sugars 8.4 g	
Total Fat 3.1 g	5%	Protein 1.1 g	
Saturated Fat 1.0 g	5%	Vitamin A	0%
Trans Fat		Vitamin C	0%
Cholesterol 7mg	2%	Calcium	2%
Sodium 5mg	0%	Iron	4%

Angel Food Cake

Total Calories Per Serving: 121

They don't call it "Angel Food" for nothing. This heavenly, light dessert can be spruced up with fresh berries or a dollop of whipped cream and still be more saintly than sinful for your dieting!

Ingredients

1 cup cake flour
¾ cup sugar
1½ teaspoons vanilla
½ teaspoon almond extract

12 large egg whites, at room
   temperature
1½ teaspoons cream of tartar
¼ teaspoon salt
¾ cup sugar

Directions

Step 1: Preheat oven to 375°.

Step 2: In a medium sized bowl, sift together the flour and sugar and set aside.

Step 3: In a small bowl, whisk together the vanilla extract and almond extract and set aside.

Step 4: In a third, large, mixing bowl, beat together the egg whites, cream of tartar, and salt until the mixture begins to form peaks.

Step 5: Slowly whisk the extracts, then the flour and sugar into this mixture.

Step 6: Pour into an ungreased tube pan and bake 30 to 35 minutes. Remove from oven and immediately remove cake from pan. Set on a cooling rack and let cool about 2 hours before serving.

Nutritional Information

Calories 121		Total Carbohydrates 26.7 g	9%
Calories from Fat 1		Dietary Fiber	
	% Daily Value	Sugars 8.4 g	
Total Fat 0.1 g	0%	Protein 1.1 g	
Saturated Fat		Vitamin A	0%
Trans Fat		Vitamin C	0%
Cholesterol 0mg	0%	Calcium	0%
Sodium 76mg	3%	Iron	2%

Sweet Spicy Apples

Total Calories Per Serving: 128

Apple-cinnamon fans will revel in this simple way to spice up apples. This is a nice dessert, for sure, but you may also consider serving it as a side to a plainly prepared pork loin steak or chicken breast to create a spicy and satisfyingly sweet low-calorie meal.

Makes 8 Servings

Ingredients

8 apples
2 tablespoons white sugar
1 teaspoon lemon juice
¼ cup cinnamon
1 tablespoon butter, melted

Directions

Step 1: Heat oven to 375°.
Step 2: Peel and core apples, and slice into wedge-like chunks.
Step 3: In a bowl, toss apples with sugar, cinnamon, and butter, until fully coated.
Step 4: Bake 25 to 30 minutes, until apples are softened and nicely browned. Serve warm.

Nutritional Information

Calories 128		Total Carbohydrates 31.1 g	10%
Calories from Fat 13		Dietary Fiber 6.2 g	25%
	% Daily Value	Sugars 22.1 g	
Total Fat 1.5 g	2%	Protein 0.2 gg	
Saturated Fat 0.9 g	5%	Vitamin A	3%
Trans Fat		Vitamin C	15%
Cholesterol 4mg	1%	Calcium	5%
Sodium 13mg	1%	Iron	3%

Fruit Sorbet

Total Calories Per Serving: 130

This fruit sorbet recipe calls for mango, but sorbets can be made from any fruit you like. Once you get the process down, experiment with other fruits for a sweet, refreshing treat.

Makes 6 Servings

Ingredients

2 mangos, peeled and cut into cubes
½ cup simple syrup
1½ tablespoons fresh lime juice

Directions

Step 1: Place fruit into a food processor or blender and blend until puréed.
Step 2: Pour in syrup and lime juice and pulse until smooth.
Step 3: Pour into an ice cream maker and freeze.

Note: If you don't have an ice cream maker, you can still make this sorbet (and ice cream). Here's how: Once the sorbet ingredients are fully blended, pour them in a bowl, cover, and refrigerate for an hour. Next, move to the freezer for an hour. Remove from freezer, beat with an electric mixer for three minutes, and return to freezer. Repeat this process 3 or 4 more times, and freeze overnight.

Nutritional Information

Calories 130		Total Carbohydrates 34.1 g	11%
Calories from Fat 3		Dietary Fiber 1.4 g	5%
	% Daily Value	Sugars 10.4 g	
Total Fat 0.3 g	1%	Protein 0.4 g	
Saturated Fat		Vitamin A	11%
Trans Fat		Vitamin C	34%
Cholesterol 0mg	0%	Calcium	1%
Sodium 20mg	1%	Iron	1%

Easy and Natural "Fruit Sticks"

Total Calories Per Serving: 70

Tell your kids they're having fruit sticks for dessert and they will no doubt imagine some factory-processed, fruit-flavored, textured-like-plastic confectionary in colorful, cartoonish packaging. But the presentation of these fruit kebabs is so colorful and stunning they might not be so disappointed when they learn this is what you meant!

Makes 5 Servings

Ingredients

 5 large strawberries, halved
 ¼ cantaloupe, cut into balls or cubes
 2 bananas, peeled and cut into chunks
 1 apple, cut into chunks
 20 skewers

Directions

Step 1: Thread the strawberries, cantaloupe, banana, and apple pieces alternately onto skewers, placing at least 2 pieces of each fruit on each skewer.

Step 2: Arrange the fruit skewers decoratively on a serving platter.

Note: You can also use honeydew, pineapple, kiwi, mango, blueberries, raspberries, or whatever fruits your family most enjoys.

Nutritional Information

Calories 70		Total Carbohydrates 17.8 g	6%
Calories from Fat 2		Dietary Fiber 2.4 g	10%
	% Daily Value	Sugars 11.1 g	
Total Fat 0.2 g	0%	Protein 0.7 g	
Saturated Fat	0%	Vitamin A	6%
Trans Fat		Vitamin C	34%
Cholesterol 0mg	0%	Calcium	1%
Sodium 2mg	0%	Iron	1%

Five-Fruit Bake

Total Calories Per Serving: 160

A sumptuous treat for fruit lovers—and only 160 calories per serving! Enjoy with a small scoop of vanilla ice cream for a special treat.

Ingredients

6 peaches, chopped
3 pears, peeled and chopped
4 stalks rhubarb, sliced
2 tablespoons raisins
3 red delicious apples, peeled and chopped
2 tablespoons biscuit mix
¼ cup light brown sugar
1 tablespoon butter, softened

Directions

Step 1: Preheat oven to 375°. Spray an ovenproof glass casserole dish with cooking spray.

Step 2: In a large bowl, toss together the peaches, pears, rhubarb slices, raisins, and apples, until nicely combined. Pour into the baking dish and distribute evenly.

Step 3: In another bowl, mix together the baking mix, brown sugar, and butter, until the mixture becomes crumbly in texture. Pour this mixture over the fruit.

Step 4: Place in oven and bake 45 minutes, until the top is golden brown. Serve warm.

Nutritional Information

Calories 160		Total Carbohydrates 33.7 g	11%
Calories from Fat 26		Dietary Fiber 4.4 g	17%
	% Daily Value	Sugars 20.4 g	
Total Fat 2.9 g	4%	Protein 2.2 g	
Saturated Fat 0.5 g	3%	Vitamin A	17%
Trans Fat		Vitamin C	64%
Cholesterol 0mg	0%	Calcium	5%
Sodium 154mg	6%	Iron	5%

"Chocolate" Crepes

Total Calories Per Serving: 143

Nutella takes the place of chocolate filling in these yummy crepes, making them just a wee bit healthier and giving them an extra level of flavor with hazelnut. The crepe shells can be made ahead and refrigerated, filling them when you're ready to enjoy them.

Makes 15 Crepes

Ingredients

2 eggs
½ cup milk
½ cup water
¾ cup all-purpose flour
6 teaspoons white sugar

1 teaspoon butter
1 ounce cognac
8 ounces Nutella spread
Powdered sugar (optional)

Directions

Step 1: Whisk together the eggs, milk, water, flour, sugar, butter, and cognac in a medium sized bowl until all the ingredients are nicely combined.

Step 2: Heat a nonstick skillet to high and spoon enough batter into the pan so that it just covers the bottom. Swirl the batter around if you need to and make sure there are no holes. If there are, fill before the batter sets. (It will set quickly.)

Step 3: Cook the crepe only about a minute before gently flipping with a rubber spatula.

Step 4: Cook the other side about 30 seconds and slide from pan. Repeat until you run out of batter.

Step 5: Stack the crepes to cool, about 15 to 20 minutes.

Step 6: To fill, spread out about a tablespoon of Nutella about a quarter of the way in on one side of the crepe. Roll with your fingers and plate, seam side down. Sprinkle with powdered sugar, if desired, and serve. Repeat for remaining crepes; refrigerate those not used for 2 to 3 days.

Nutritional Information

Calories 143		Total Carbohydrates 17.8 g	6%
Calories from Fat 56		Dietary Fiber 1.1 g	4%
	% Daily Value	Sugars 11.6 g	
Total Fat 6.3 g	10%	Protein 2.6 g	
Saturated Fat 1.4 g	7%	Vitamin A	9%
Trans Fat		Vitamin C	0%
Cholesterol 23mg	8%	Calcium	0%
Sodium 21mg	1%	Iron	2%

Avocado Chocolate Pudding

Total Calories Per Serving: 132

Avocado lovers rejoice! You are not going to believe how wonderful your beloved creamy fruit goes with banana and chocolate in this decadent, easy-to-make pudding.

Make 4-6 Servings

Ingredients
1 ripe avocado
4 bananas
¼ cup unsweetened cocoa powder

Directions
Step 1: Extract the meat from the avocado and place in a blender. Discard pit and skin.
Step 2: Peel and break up the four bananas and toss them into the blender.
Step 3: Start pulsing the avocado and banana together, then add the cocoa.
Step 4: Blend until all ingredients meld and the pudding is smooth. Remove from blender and pour into a bowl. Refrigerate for 1 hour, then serve and enjoy.

Nutritional Information

Calories 132		Total Carbohydrates 22.8 g	8%
Calories from Fat 51		Dietary Fiber 5.5 g	22%
	% Daily Value	Sugars 9.9 g	
Total Fat 5.7 g	9%	Protein 2.2 g	
Saturated Fat 1.1 g	5%	Vitamin A	2%
Trans Fat		Vitamin C	17%
Cholesterol 0mg	0%	Calcium	1%
Sodium 4mg	0%	Iron	5%

Low-Cal and Luscious Chocolate Almond Pudding

Total Calories Per Serving: 103

Creamy, chocolatey goodness, simply made for about 100 calories. How could you go wrong? As an extra-specially decadent treat, serve with a dollop of homemade whipped cream (see page 168) and enjoy!

Makes 4-6 Servings

Ingredients

½ cup sugar
⅓ cup baking cocoa
2 tablespoons cornstarch
2 cups milk

1 egg, beaten
¼ teaspoon vanilla extract
⅛ teaspoon almond extract

Directions

Step 1: Set a medium saucepan on the stove to medium heat.
Step 2: In a bowl, mix together the sugar, cocoa, and cornstarch. Add to pan.
Step 3: Whisk together milk and eggs, then pour into the pan with the dry ingredients and lightly fold the ingredients together.
Step 4: Continue mixing while the pudding comes to boil and keep cooking and constantly stirring as it thickens into a pudding.
Step 5: Now remove the pan from the heat and stir in the vanilla and almond extract. Serve warm, or, if desired, remove to another bowl, refrigerate at least two hours, and serve chilled.

Nutritional Information

Calories 103		Total Carbohydrates 19.2 g	6%
Calories from Fat 20		Dietary Fiber 1.2 g	5%
	% Daily Value	Sugars 15.7 g	
Total Fat 2.2 g	6%	Protein 3.4 g	
Saturated Fat		Vitamin A	1%
Trans Fat		Vitamin C	0%
Cholesterol 25mg	8%	Calcium	1%
Sodium 34mg	1%	Iron	3%

METRIC AND IMPERIAL CONVERSIONS

(These conversions are rounded for convenience)

Ingredient	Cups/Tablespoons/Teaspoons	Ounces	Grams/Milliliters
Butter	1 cup=16 tablespoons= 2 sticks	8 ounces	230 grams
Cream cheese	1 tablespoon	0.5 ounce	14.5 grams
Cheese, shredded	1 cup	4 ounces	110 grams
Cornstarch	1 tablespoon	0.3 ounce	8 grams
Flour, all-purpose	1 cup/1 tablespoon	4.5 ounces/0.3 ounce	125 grams/8 grams
Flour, whole wheat	1 cup	4 ounces	120 grams
Fruit, dried	1 cup	4 ounces	120 grams
Fruits or veggies, chopped	1 cup	5 to 7 ounces	145 to 200 grams
Fruits or veggies, pureed	1 cup	8.5 ounces	245 grams
Honey, maple syrup, or corn syrup	1 tablespoon	.75 ounce	20 grams
Liquids: cream, milk, water, or juice	1 cup	8 fluid ounces	240 milliliters
Oats	1 cup	5.5 ounces	150 grams
Salt	1 teaspoon	0.2 ounces	6 grams
Spices: cinnamon, cloves, ginger, or nutmeg (ground)	1 teaspoon	0.2 ounce	5 milliliters
Sugar, brown, firmly packed	1 cup	7 ounces	200 grams
Sugar, white	1 cup/1 tablespoon	7 ounces/0.5 ounce	200 grams/12.5 grams
Vanilla extract	1 teaspoon	0.2 ounce	4 grams

OVEN TEMPERATURES

Fahrenheit	Celcius	Gas Mark
225°	110°	¼
250°	120°	½
275°	140°	1
300°	150°	2
325°	160°	3
350°	180°	4
375°	190°	5
400°	200°	6
425°	220°	7
450°	230°	8